The Dhammapada

The Dhammapada

The Sayings of the Buddha

A bilingual edition in Pāḷi and English

Translated and with an introduction by

Ānandajoti Bhikkhu

evertype

2019

Published by Evertype, 19A Corso Street, Dundee, DD2 1DR, Scotland. www.evertype.com.

Editor: Michael Everson.

A catalogue record for this book is available from the British Library.

ISBN-10 1-78201-258-3
ISBN-13 978-1-78201-258-0

Typeset in Baskerville and New Pelican by Michael Everson.

Design and cover design: Michael Everson. “Asian lotus background” © Veyronik. https://www.dreamstime.com/veyronik_info.

Preface

It is a great pleasure to have prepared for publication a new edition of the Dhammapada, one of the most central texts of Theravāda Buddhism. In particular it is pleasant to do so in a bilingual edition, convenient for students of Pāḷi, which I first encountered as a post-graduate student in Los Angeles many years ago.

It has likewise been a pleasure communicating with Ānandajoti Bhikkhu as the edition was being prepared. He was generous with his encouragement and responsive to my queries. Of his two translations of the Dhammapada, I have favoured the more scholarly of the two, though I appreciate the aesthetic of the metrical qualities of the more popular translation.

I have made a very few alterations to Ānandajoti's translation, with his consent and approval. Firstly, I have preferred the Sanskrit terms *arhat*, *Dharma*, *gandharva*, *Gautama*, and *Nirvana* since these have long been accepted loanwords in English while *arahant*, *Dhamma*, *gandhabba*, *Gotama*, and *Nibbana* are (rightly or wrongly) not; I prefer the accented form *Nirvāṇa* and *Nibbāna* in a book such as this though. Secondly, I have preferred to use the definite article when the text refers to "the Dharma" since this seems to be the most conventional for Buddhist discourse in English. Thirdly, I replaced the superscript ^{a} and ^{i} used by Ānandajoti for reduced vowels with *a̭* and *i̭* because it seems to me to be more legible in a print publication (see the discussion on page xi). Lastly, I have favoured Oxford spelling and the Oxford comma where applicable.

Like Ānandajoti, I trust that this edition will find favour with students of the Dharma, as well as with students of Pāḷi, a rich and subtle language.

Michael Everson
Dundee, December 2019

Introduction:
A Book of Ethical Teachings

The Dhammapada is probably the most popular book in the Pāḷi Canon, and has had innumerable translations into most modern languages.[1] The timeless ethical teachings contained in these verses are still considered relevant to people's lives, and they are a good guide to living well, and show how to reap the rewards of good living.

Together with the commentarial stories that accompany the verses—along with the Jātaka verses and stories—they have formed the backbone of the teaching of Buddhist ethics for well over 2,000 years. The verses and stories are well known in traditional Theravāda Buddhist cultures, and most born and brought up in those societies will be able to recite many of the verses, and relate the stories that go with them, even from a young age.

This is not at all surprising as the verses are often memorable, and the stories that accompany them equally so.[2] They provided a framework for understanding what are good and bad actions, and what the consequences of both will be, which is central to the Buddhist teaching on ethics.

The popularity of the stories can be seen from the many times they are found illustrated on the ancient monuments of India, especially around *cetiyas*;[3] they are also seen in frescoes and reliefs in temples in Buddhist countries right up to the present day, and they serve to remind and reinforce the teachings that they embody.

The collection consists of 423 verses, organized into twenty-six chapters, most of which are fairly short. As there are something like 20,000 verses in the Pāḷi Canon,[4] this is but a very small collection and the Dhammapada is indeed one of the smallest books in the Canon.[5] Most of the verses stand

1 Including those that are no longer—or never were—homes to Buddhist cultures.

2 The commentarial stories, which give the background to the verses, can be found in Burlingame's translation can be found at www.ancient-buddhist-texts.net/English-Texts/Buddhist-Legends/, retrieved 2019-11-22.

3 Sanskrit *caitya*, a kind of memorial; the architectural form is usually a *stūpa*.

4 Around 140 of the verses have parallels elsewhere in the Canon.

5 Only Khuddakapāṭha, which appears to have been added much later than the other texts, and Cariyāpiṭaka, also a late text, are shorter.

by themselves, although in some cases they come in pairs,[6] and in others two or more verses are evidently joined together to form a longer unit.

The verses give instruction to the different groups that comprise the Buddhist community, including advice for the lay person and the monastic, and a number of the verses, especially towards the end, show ways for understanding who is living up to their role in the community well, and who is not.[7]

Types of verse

The verses I think could well be described as primitive, in the sense that they lack the refinements and elaboration of high classical Indian verse, and their directness is also part of their charm.

I have identified certain basic types of verse that have been used in the Dhammapada, and classified them according to whether they are descriptive,[8] prescriptive, or rhetorical verses (such as questions and so forth). Further the verses employ similes and metaphors in making their teachings memorable.

Of course the verses do not adhere strictly to one type or another, and there are some overlaps, but this does seem to summaries their contents fairly well. Below I give lists showing where these occur in the text.

Descriptive verses simple state the facts as they were understood by the Buddha, or by the early Buddhist community. An example might be the opening verse of the collection:

1 **Manopubbaṅgamā dhammā, manoseṭṭhā manomayā,**
Mind precedes thoughts, mind is their chief,
(their quality is) made by mind,
manasā ce paduṭṭhena bhāsati vā karoti vā,
if with a base mind one speaks or acts,
tato naṁ dukkham-anveti cakkaṁ va vahato padaṁ.
through that suffering follows him like a wheel (follows) the ox's foot.

There are around 344 verses of this type (81%): 1–39, 41, 42, 43, 45, 46, 47, 48, 51–60, 63–74, 76, 79–83, 86, 89–115, 117–122, 124–128, 131, 132, 134–145, 148–156, 160–165, 171–178, 181–196, 200–209, 211, 217–220,

6 Most notably in the first chapter.
7 I think particularly of the Chapters on Monastics and Brahmins here.
8 These often have prescriptive force in that they describe correct behaviour, without, however, saying that you should follow it.

222, 225–230, 235, 237, 240, 241, 244–247, 249–263, 265–273, 275–280, 283, 284, 286, 287, 288, 291–301, 303–312, 314–326, 331–339, 341, 342, 346, 347, 349–352, 354–368, 372–375, 378, 381, 382, 384–388, 390–393, 395–323.

Prescriptive verses actually lay down rules for behaviour, or recommend a course of action as being more beneficial. An example is the 40th verse of the collection:

40 **Kumbhūpamaṁ kāyam-imaṁ viditvā,**
Knowing this body is (frail) like a jar,
nagarūpamaṁ cittam-idaṁ ṭhapetvā,
establishing the mind like a fortress,
yodhetha Māraṁ paññāvudhena,
fight Māra with the weapon of wisdom,
jitañ-ca rakkhe, anivesano siyā.
guard your success, and do not be attached.

I count 67 verses as belonging to this category (15%): 40, 46, 49, 50, 61, 75, 77, 78, 84, 87, 88, 116, 123, 129, 130, 133, 144, 157, 158, 159, 166, 167, 168, 169, 170, 197, 198, 199, 210, 221, 223, 224, 231, 232, 233, 234, 236, 238, 239, 242, 243, 248, 274, 281, 282, 285, 289, 290, 302, 313, 315, 327, 328, 329, 330, 340, 343, 348, 369, 370, 371, 376, 377, 379, 380, 383, 389.

There are only 13 **Rhetorical** verses by my reckoning, and they make up 3% of the collection. Verse 44 is an example:

44 **Kŏ imaṁ paṭhaviṁ vicessati**
Who will know this earth
yamalokañ-ca imaṁ sadevakaṁ?
and the lower realm, together with the gods?
Ko dhammapadaṁ sudesitaṁ
Who (will reflect) on the well-taught verse of the Dharma
kusalo puppham-ivappacessati?
as a good man reflects on a flower?

See verses 44, 46, 62, 146, 179, 180, 212–216, 264, 353, 394.

Similes,[9] in which otherwise unlike things are compared to drive home a point, are used in many places throughout the collection. An example is found in the last pair of lines in verse 7, which compares the ease with which Māra can overthrow the indolent to the way a weak tree is easily overthrown by the wind:

7 **Subhānupassiṁ viharantaṁ, indriyesu asaṁvutaṁ,**
Living contemplating what is pleasant,
uncontrolled in sense faculties,
bhojanamhi amattaññuṁ, kusītaṁ hīnavīriyaṁ –
not knowing the limit in food, indolent, low in energy—
taṁ ve pasahati Māro vāto rukkhaṁ va dubbalaṁ.
Māra surely overthrows that one, like wind (overthrows) a weak tree.

There are 89 verses employing similes (21%): 1, 2, 7, 8, 13, 14, 19, 21, 28, 29, 31, 33, 34, 40, 44, 45, 46, 49, 51, 52, 53, 58, 59, 64, 65, 71, 76, 81, 82, 91–95, 123, 125, 134, 135, 136, 143, 144, 149, 150, 152, 155, 156, 161, 162, 164, 170–174, 202, 208, 219, 220, 222, 235, 239, 240, 251, 252, 268, 284, 285, 287, 304, 311, 315, 320, 325, 326, 327, 329, 330, 334–338, 342, 343, 347, 377, 380, 401, 407, 413.

Metaphors do not use comparison, but suggest a resemblance between otherwise disparate objects. An example can be found in verse 25, where the island is the safe haven the person who is striving hopes to make.

25 **Uṭṭhānen' appamādena saṁyamena damena ca,**
Through activity, heedfulness, through self-control,
and through restraint,
dīpaṁ kayirātha medhāvī yaṁ ogho nābhikīrati.
the sage should make an island that no flood waters can overcome.

I identify 77 verses in this collection that use metaphors (18%): 25, 26, 35, 40, 46, 47, 48, 54–57, 60, 66, 69, 80, 85, 86, 103, 121, 122, 145, 147, 151, 153, 154, 160, 174, 175, 204, 205, 211, 218, 222, 235–238, 242–244, 254, 255, 262, 263, 275, 276, 282, 283, 288, 294, 295, 302, 321–323, 339–341, 344–346, 350, 351, 354, 356–359, 363, 369–371, 385, 387, 388, 414.

9 Normally signified by a comparison word such as *iva*, *va*, *viya*, *yathā*, *upama*, and *sama*.

Layout

Most of the verses are written in the Siloka metre, which has four lines of eight syllables to the line. As the semantic unit is normally a pair of lines, they are laid out in the text as two pairs of lines.

In the Dhammapada there are quite a few verses written in other metrical structures, which include Tuṭṭhubha (11 syllables), Jagati (12 syllables), Vetālīya, and Opacchandasaka (both variable in length).[10]

These are set out as four separate lines, matching the semantic unit, which here is normally the line. An example of Vetālīya metre (v. 15):

15 **Idha socati, pecca socati,**
Here he laments, after death he laments,
pāpakārī ubhayattha socati,
the wicked one laments in both places,
so socati, so vihaññati,
he laments, he suffers vexation,
disvā kammakiliṭṭham-attano.
seeing the defilement of his own deeds.

An example of Tuṭṭhubha metre (v. 19):

19 **Bahum-pi ce sahitaṁ bhāsamāno,**
Even though reciting abundant scriptures,
na takkaro hoti naro pamatto,
the heedless fellow, who does not do (what they say),
gopo va gāvo gaṇayaṁ paresaṁ,
like a cowboy counting other's cattle,
na bhāgavā sāmaññassa hoti.
does not partake of the ascetic life.

In this translation normally I take one verse at a time, but occasionally when a verse is connected intimately to the next verse or verses, and they cannot be separated, half-brackets are used with the verse numbers to show the relation. An example (verses 58–59):

58⌝ **Yathā saṅkāradhānasmiṁ ujjhitasmiṁ mahāpathe**
Just as in a forsaken and discarded heap along the highway

10 For more details of the metre see my *New Edition of the Dhammapada*: www.ancient-buddhist-texts.net/Buddhist-Texts/K2-Dhammapada-New/, retrieved 2019-11-22.

padumaṁ tattha jāyetha, sucigandhaṁ manoramaṁ,
a lotus might arise in that place, with a pure fragrance,
delighting the mind,

59⌋ **evaṁ saṅkārabhūtesu, andhabhūte puthujjane**
° so amongst the forsaken, the Perfect Sambuddha's disciple
atirocati paññāya Sammāsambuddhasāvako.
outshines the blind and ordinary folk through his wisdom.

Verses joined in this way include: 58–59, 73–74, 85–86, 104–105, 137–140, 153–154, 186–187, 188–189, 190–192, 195–196, 219–220, 229–230, 242–243, 246–247, 262–263, 271–272, 345–346, 360–361.

Conventions

Normally I translate the Pāḷi line-by-line, but if two lines have to be taken together for translation, then I usually mark the line with a small circle ° at the beginning of the first line, to indicate that this has been done.

An example (v. 35):

35 **Dunniggahassa lahuno yatthakāmanipātino,**
° For the mind that is difficult to subdue, flighty,
flitting wherever it will,
cittassa damatho sādhu, cittaṁ dantaṁ sukhāvahaṁ.
restraint is good, a restrained mind brings happiness.

Here, *For the mind* in the first line of the English translates *cittassa* in the second line of the Pāḷi. Verses affected in this way are: 35, 37, 47, 48, 57, 59, 164, 180, 188, 208, 267, 284, 341, 345, 388, 405, 409.

Occasionally in the Pāḷi either the vowel *a* or the vowel *i* will be written with a small inverted breve below (as in *kayi̯rā* and *ara̯hati*); this is done when the vowel employed is written but should not be pronounced with its full length, owing to the need to fit the metre. An example (v. 22):

22 **Etaṁ visesato ñatvā appamādamhi paṇḍitā,**
The wise, understanding this difference in regard to heedfulness,
appamāde pamodanti, Ari̯yānaṁ gocare ratā.
rejoice in heedfulness, delight in the domain of the Noble Ones.

Verses affected in this way are (*a̮*): 8, 9, 10, 30, 82, 95, 98, 230, 389, and (*i̮*): 22, 25, 42, 43, 53, 61 ×2, 64, 65, 73, 79, 88, 105, 112, 117 ×3, 118 ×2, 141, 155, 156, 159, 161, 164, 177, 183, 190, 191, 206, 208, 211, 223, 267, 281, 292, 312, 313, 330, 388.

Occasionally the vowel *e* or the vowel *o* is marked with a breve; again this is because of the metre, which in this place demands that a syllable that is normally heavy be counted as a light syllable. An example (v. 44):

44 **Kŏ imaṁ paṭhaviṁ vicessati**
Who will know this earth
yamalokañ-ca imaṁ sadevakaṁ?
and the lower realm, together with the gods?

Verses affected in this way are (*ĕ*): 17, 18, and (*ŏ*): 44, 95, 172, 173, 324, 341, 362 ×2, 382.

Online editions

My translation of the Dhammapada has been published online at www.ancient-buddhist-texts.net in two different editions. The more scholarly of the two, which has been used for the translation in this book, is the version found in the Texts and Translations section of the website.[11] It discusses the grammar and the interpretation of the text, and matters connected with the collecting and positioning of the verses in the text, and occasionally shows how the text could have been better written. On the website pages I have also collected related verses from the Dhammapada collection at the end of each chapter.

The second translation is a more popular presentation, placed in the English section of the website.[12] This includes giving a moral to the verse, followed by a synopsis of the commentarial story, the verse in Pāḷi, and then a metrical translation. The model for this work was my previous Buddhist Wisdom Verses, which contained around fifty of the verses from the Dhammapada.

These texts are the culmination of nearly 15 years of work on the Pāḷi Dhammapada, and were preceded by a number of other texts, listed below.

11 www.ancient-buddhist-texts.net/Texts-and-Translations/Dhammapada/, accessed on 2019-11-22.

12 www.ancient-buddhist-texts.net/English-Texts/Dhamma-Verses/, accessed on 2019-11-22.

They give information supplementary to the texts presented here, which I have not repeated in this edition.

The first I worked on was the Romanized transliteration of the Sinhala-letter *Buddha Jayantī Tripiṭaka Granthamālā* text which I prepared around 2002–2003. That work set in motion a study of the text that led first to a *New Edition of the Dhammapada* in 2004,[13] which compared the variants in the major printed editions of the Pāḷi text, and also took into consideration the metre. For variant readings and metrical analysis, that is the edition to refer to.

That work then formed the basis for *A Comparative Edition of the Dhammapada*,[14] which brought together all the known parallels in Middle Indo-Aryan languages, together with studies and extensive indexes. There you will find the same verse, or parts of a verse, given in the ancient languages which were cognate to the Pāḷi, but it is for the advanced student only.

In 2017 when I began work on the Dhammapada translations, I extracted the information from the latter work, and added more to it, listing all the parallels in the Pāḷi Canonical and para-Canonical literature, as well as in other Middle Indo-Aryan languages.[15]

Other works which have been connected to the Dhammapada include publishing online Margaret Cone's *Patna Dhammapada*, with studies, metrical analysis and indexes;[16] and Franz Bernhard's *Udānavarga*,[17] in which I made similar additions.

13 See note 10 above.

14 www.ancient-buddhist-texts.net/Buddhist-Texts/C3-Comparative-Dhammapada/, retrieved 2019-11-22.

15 www.ancient-buddhist-texts.net/Buddhist-Texts/K2-Dhammapada-Parallels/, retrieved 2019-11-22.

16 www.ancient-buddhist-texts.net/Buddhist-Texts/C5-Patna/, retrieved 2019-11-22.

17 www.ancient-buddhist-texts.net/Buddhist-Texts/S1-Udanavarga/, retrieved 2019-11-22.

Acknowledgements

I am grateful to Ayyā Sudhammā, who went through the text very diligently, and with humour and patience pointed out its manifold shortcomings. I have now managed to remove some of those, but any that remain are of course entirely my own fault.

I hope this work will help to continue the great tradition of providing moral guidance to the present generation in a form that they can find clear and appealing. Any merit accruing form this work I would like to dedicate to my parents: may they be well and happy and peaceful in their new lives.

Ānandajoti Bhikkhu
Sadao, Songkhla, Thailand, November 2019

The Dhammapada

Sūcipatta

1 Yamakavaggo (1–20) 4
2 Appamādavaggo (21–32) 12
3 Cittavaggo (33–43) 16
4 Pupphavaggo (44–59) 20
5 Bālavaggo (60–75) 26
6 Paṇḍitavaggo (76–89) 32
7 Arahantavaggo (90–99) 38
8 Sahassavaggo (100–115) 42
9 Pāpavaggo (116–128) 48
10 Daṇḍavaggo (129–145) 54
11 Jarāvaggo (146–156) 60
12 Attavaggo (157–166) 64
13 Lokavaggo (167–178) 68
14 Buddhavaggo (179–196) 72
15 Sukhavaggo (197–208) 78
16 Piyavaggo (209–220) 82
17 Kodhavaggo (221–234) 86
18 Malavaggo (235–255) 92
19 Dhammaṭṭhavaggo (256–272) 98
20 Maggavaggo (273–289) 104
21 Pakiṇṇakavaggo (290–305) 110
22 Nirayavaggo (306–319) 116
23 Nāgavaggo (320–333) 122
24 Taṇhāvaggo (334–359) 128
25 Bhikkhuvaggo (360–382) 138
26 Brāhmaṇavaggo (383–423) 146

Table of contents

1 The Chapter about the Pairs (1–20) 5
2 The Chapter about Heedfulness (21–32) 13
3 The Chapter about the Mind (33–43) 17
4 The Chapter about Flowers (44–59) 21
5 The Chapter about Fools (60–75) 27
6 The Chapter about the Wise (76–89) 33
7 The Chapter about the Arhats (90–99) 39
8 The Chapter about the Thousands (100–115) 43
9 The Chapter about Wickedness (116–128) 49
10 The Chapter about the Stick (129–145) 55
11 The Chapter about Old Age (146–156) 61
12 The Chapter about the Self (157–166) 65
13 The Chapter about the World (167–178) 69
14 The Chapter about the Buddha (179–196) 73
15 The Chapter about Happiness (197–208) 79
16 The Chapter about Love (209–220) 83
17 The Chapter about Anger (221–234) 87
18 The Chapter about Stains (235–255) 93
19 The Chapter about One who stands by the Dharma (256–272) . . . 99
20 The Chapter about the Path (273–289) 105
21 The Miscellaneous Chapter (290–305) 111
22 The Chapter about the Underworld (306–319) 117
23 The Chapter about the Elephant (320–333) 123
24 The Chapter about Craving (334–359) 129
25 The Chapter about Monastics (360–382) 139
26 The Chapter about Brahmins (383–423) 147

1

Yamakavaggo

1 Manopubbaṅgamā dhammā, manoseṭṭhā manomayā,
manasā ce– paduṭṭhena bhāsati vā karoti vā,
tato naṁ dukkham-anveti cakkaṁ va vahato padaṁ.

2 Manopubbaṅgamā dhammā, manoseṭṭhā manomayā,
manasā ce pasannena bhāsati vā karoti vā,
tato naṁ sukham-anveti chāyā va anapāyinī.

3 "Akkocchi maṁ, avadhi maṁ, ajini maṁ, ahāsi me",
ye ca taṁ upanayhanti, veraṁ tesaṁ na sammati.

4 "Akkocchi maṁ, avadhi maṁ, ajini maṁ, ahāsi me",
ye taṁ na upanayhanti, veraṁ tesūpasammati.

5 Na hi verena verāni sammantīdha kudācanaṁ,
averena ca sammanti, esa dhammo sanantano.

1

The Chapter about the Pairs

1 Mind precedes thoughts, mind is their chief,
(their quality is) made by mind,
if with a base mind one speaks or acts,
through that suffering follows him like a wheel (follows) the ox's foot.

2 Mind precedes thoughts, mind is their chief,
(their quality is) made by mind,
if with pure mind one speaks or acts,
through that happiness follows him
like a shadow which does not depart.

3 "He abused me, he struck at me, he overcame me, he robbed me,"
those who bear ill-will towards this their hatred is never appeased.

4 "He abused me, he struck at me, he overcame me, he robbed me,"
those who do not bear ill-will towards this their hatred is appeased.

5 For not by hatred do hatreds cease at any time in this place,
they only cease with non-hatred, this truth is (surely) eternal.

6 Pare ca na vijānanti mayam-ettha yamāmase,
ye ca tattha vijānanti tato sammanti medhagā.

7 Subhānupassiṁ viharantaṁ, indriyesu asaṁvutaṁ,
bhojanamhi amattaññuṁ, kusītaṁ hīnavīriyaṁ—
taṁ ve pasahati Māro vāto rukkhaṁ va dubbalaṁ.

8 Asubhānupassiṁ viharantaṁ, indriyesu susaṁvutaṁ,
bhojanamhi ca mattaññuṁ, saddhaṁ āraddhavīriyaṁ—
taṁ ve nappasahati Māro vāto selaṁ va pabbataṁ.

9 Anikkasāvo kāsāvaṁ yo vatthaṁ paridahessati,
apeto damasaccena na so kāsāvam-arahati.

10 Yo ca vantakasāvassa, sīlesu susamāhito,
upeto damasaccena sa ve kāsāvam-arahati.

11 Asāre sāramatino, sāre cāsāradassino,
te sāraṁ nādhigacchanti, micchāsaṅkappagocarā.

12 Sārañ-ca sārato ñatvā, asārañ-ca asārato,
te sāraṁ adhigacchanti, sammāsaṅkappagocarā.

6 The others do not understand that we should restrain ourselves here,
but (for) those here who do understand,
through that, (their) dissensions do cease.

7 Living contemplating what is pleasant,
uncontrolled in sense faculties,
not knowing the limit in food, indolent, low in energy—
Māra surely overthrows that one, like wind (overthrows) a weak tree.

8 Living contemplating the unpleasant,
well-controlled in sense faculties,
and knowing the limit in food, faithful, with energy aroused—
Māra does not overthrow that one,
just as wind does not (overthrow) a mountain made of rock.

9 The one who, while still impure, would wear the renunciant's robe,
unendowed with restraint and truth,
is not worthy of the renunciant's robe.

10 The one who, steady in virtue, throws out (any) impurity,
endowed with restraint and truth,
is indeed worthy of the renunciant's robe.

11 Finding the essential in the unessential,
and seeing the unessential in the essential,
they do not understand what is the essential,
and resort to wrong intention.

12 Knowing the essential in what is essential,
and the unessential in what is unessential,
they understand what is essential, and resort to right intention.

13 Yathā agāraṁ ducchannaṁ vuṭṭhī samativijjhati,
evaṁ abhāvitaṁ cittaṁ rāgo samativijjhati.

14 Yathā agāraṁ succhannaṁ vuṭṭhī na samativijjhati,
evaṁ subhāvitaṁ cittaṁ rāgo na samativijjhati.

15 Idha socati, pecca socati,
pāpakārī ubhayattha socati,
so socati, so vihaññati,
disvā kammakiliṭṭham-attano.

16 Idha modati, pecca modati,
katapuñño ubhayattha modati,
so modati, so pamodati,
disvā kammavisuddhim-attano.

17 Idha tappati, pecca tappati,
pāpakārī ubhayattha tappati,
"Pāpaṁ mĕ katan"-ti tappati,
bhiyyo tappati duggatiṁ gato.

18 Idha nandati, pecca nandati,
katapuñño ubhayattha nandati,
"Puññaṁ mĕ katan"-ti nandati,
bhiyyo nandati suggatiṁ gato.

19 Bahum-pi ce sahitaṁ bhāsamāno,
na takkaro hoti naro pamatto,
gopo va gāvo gaṇayaṁ paresaṁ,
na bhāgavā sāmaññassa hoti.

13 Just as the rain penetrates a house with thatching that is poor,
so passion penetrates a mind that is undeveloped.

14 Just as rain does not penetrate a house with thatching that is good,
so passion cannot penetrate a mind that is well-developed.

15 Here he laments, after death he laments,
the wicked one laments in both places,
he laments, he suffers vexation,
seeing the defilement of his own deeds.

16 Here he rejoices, after death he rejoices,
the meritorious one rejoices in both places,
he rejoices, he greatly rejoices,
seeing the purity of his own deeds.

17 Here he suffers, after death he suffers,
the wicked one suffers in both places,
he suffers, thinking: "I have done wickedness,"
gone to a bad fate, he suffers much more.

18 Here she is happy, after death she is happy,
the righteous one is happy in both places,
she is happy, thinking: "I have done merit,"
gone to a good fate, she is happy much more.

19 Even though reciting abundant scriptures,
the heedless fellow, who does not do (what they say),
like a cowboy counting other's cattle,
does not partake of the ascetic life.

20 Appam-pi ce sahitaṁ bhāsamāno,
Dhammassa hoti anudhammacārī,
rāgañ-ca dosañ-ca pahāya mohaṁ,
sammappajāno suvimuttacitto,
anupādiyāno idha vā huraṁ vā,
sa bhāgavā sāmaññassa hoti.

Yamakavaggo Paṭhamo

20 Even though reciting but few scriptures,
but living righteously in accordance with the Dharma,
abandoning greed, hate, and delusion,
understanding aright, with mind well-released,
that one, unattached here and hereafter,
(surely) partakes of the ascetic life.

The Chapter about the Pairs, the First

2

Appamādavaggo

21 Appamādo amatapadaṁ, pamādo maccuno padaṁ,
appamattā na mīyanti, ye pamattā yathā matā.

22 Etaṁ visesato ñatvā appamādamhi paṇḍitā,
appamāde pamodanti, Ariyānaṁ gocare ratā.

23 Te jhāyino sātatikā, niccaṁ daḷhaparakkamā,
phusanti dhīrā Nibbānaṁ, yogakkhemaṁ anuttaraṁ.

24 Uṭṭhānavato satīmato
sucikammassa nisammakārino,
saññatassa ca Dhammajīvino
appamattassa yasobhivaḍḍhati.

25 Uṭṭhānen' appamādena saṁyamena damena ca,
dīpaṁ kayirātha medhāvī yaṁ ogho nābhikīrati.

26 Pamādam-anuyuñjanti bālā dummedhino janā,
appamādañ-ca medhāvī dhanaṁ seṭṭhaṁ va rakkhati.

2

The Chapter about Heedfulness

21 Heedfulness is the deathless state, heedlessness the state of the dead,
the heedful do not die, (but) those who are heedless are as if dead.

22 The wise, understanding this difference in regard to heedfulness,
rejoice in heedfulness, delight in the domain of the Noble Ones.

23 Those who meditate all the time, constant and firm in their effort,
those wise ones reach Nirvāṇa, the unsurpassed release
from (all) bonds.

24 For he who is active, mindful,
pure in deeds, considerate,
self-controlled, living by the Dharma,
heedful, fame greatly increases.

25 Through activity, heedfulness, through self-control,
and through restraint,
the sage should make an island that no flood waters can overcome.

26 The foolish and stupid people cultivate heedlessness,
but the sagacious one guards heedfulness just as his greatest wealth.

27 Mā pamādam-anuyuñjetha mā kāmaratisanthavaṁ,
appamatto hi jhāyanto pappoti vipulaṁ sukhaṁ.

28 Pamādaṁ appamādena yadā nudati paṇḍito,
paññāpāsādam-āruyha, asoko sokiniṁ pajaṁ,
pabbataṭṭho va bhummaṭṭhe dhīro bāle avekkhati.

29 Appamatto pamattesu, suttesu bahujāgaro,
abalassaṁ va sīghasso hitvā, yāti sumedhaso.

30 Appamādena Maghavā devānaṁ seṭṭhataṁ gato,
appamādaṁ pasaṁsanti, pamādo garahito sadā.

31 Appamādarato bhikkhu, pamāde bhayadassivā,
saṁyojanaṁ aṇuṁ-thūlaṁ ḍahaṁ aggīva gacchati.

32 Appamādarato bhikkhu, pamāde bhayadassivā,
abhabbo parihānāya: Nibbānasseva santike.

Appamādavaggo Dutiyo

27 Do not cultivate heedlessness, do not be acquainted with delight in
sensual pleasure,
for the heedful one, meditating, (surely) attains great happiness.

28 When the wise one eliminates heedlessness with his heedfulness,
and mounts the palace of wisdom, griefless,
(he looks) on grieving people;
the wise one, like one standing on a mountain,
looks down on the fools, who are standing on the plains.

29 Heedful amongst the heedless ones, wakeful
amongst the ones who sleep,
like a swift horse who abandons a weak horse,
the true sage moves on.

30 Through heedfulness Maghavā attained leadership of the gods,
(the good) praise heedfulness, (but) heedlessness is always blamed.

31 A monastic who delights in heedfulness,
seeing danger in heedlessness,
advances like burning fire against the fetter, small or large.

32 A monastic who delights in heedfulness,
seeing danger in heedlessness,
is unable to fall away: he is well-nigh to Nirvāṇa.

The Chapter about Heedfulness, the Second

3

Cittavaggo

33 Phandanaṁ capalaṁ cittaṁ, dūrakkhaṁ dunnivārayaṁ,
ujuṁ karoti medhāvī, usukāro va tejanaṁ.

34 Vārijo va thale khitto, oka-m-okata ubbhato,
pariphandatidaṁ cittaṁ, Māradheyyaṁ pahātave.

35 Dunniggahassa lahuno yatthakāmanipātino,
cittassa damatho sādhu, cittaṁ dantaṁ sukhāvahaṁ.

36 Sududdasaṁ sunipuṇaṁ yatthakāmanipātinaṁ,
cittaṁ rakkhetha medhāvī, cittaṁ guttaṁ sukhāvahaṁ.

37 Dūraṅgamaṁ ekacaraṁ, asarīraṁ guhāsayaṁ,
ye cittaṁ saññam-essanti, mokkhanti Mārabandhanā.

38 Anavaṭṭhitacittassa, Saddhammaṁ avijānato,
pariplavapasādassa, paññā na paripūrati.

3
The Chapter about the Mind

33 An agitated, unsteady mind, difficult to guard, difficult to ward,
the sagacious one makes straight, as a fletcher does his arrow.

34 Like a fish thrown up on dry land, pulled out from its watery home,
the mind is agitated, (one ought) to throw off the sway of Māra.

35 ° For the mind that is difficult to subdue, flighty,
flitting wherever it will,
restraint is good, a restrained mind brings happiness.

36 Hard to see, very subtle, flitting wherever it will,
the sage should guard the mind, a guarded mind brings happiness.

37 ° Those who will restrain the mind that roams far,
is lonesome, without a body, hidden,
gain release from the bonds of Māra.

38 For the one with unsettled mind,
who does not know the True Dharma,
whose confidence is wavering, wisdom is unfulfilled.

39 Anavassutacittassa, ananvāhatacetaso,
puññapāpapahīnassa natthi jāgarato bhayaṁ.

40 Kumbhūpamaṁ kāyam-imaṁ viditvā,
nagarūpamaṁ cittam-idaṁ ṭhapetvā,
yodhetha Māraṁ paññāvudhena,
jitañ-ca rakkhe, anivesano siyā.

41 Aciraṁ vatayaṁ kāyo paṭhaviṁ adhisessati,
chuddho apetaviññāṇo, niratthaṁ va kaliṅgaraṁ.

42 Diso disaṁ yan-taṁ kayirā, verī vā pana verinaṁ—
micchāpaṇihitaṁ cittaṁ pāpiyo naṁ tato kare.

43 Na taṁ mātā pitā kayirā, aññe vā pi ca ñātakā,
sammāpaṇihitaṁ cittaṁ seyyaso naṁ tato kare.

Cittavaggo Tatiyo

39 For the one with mind free of lust,
for the one with mind unperplexed,
for the one who has abandoned making merit and demerit,
for the watchful, there is no fear.

40 Knowing this body is (frail) like a jar,
establishing the mind like a fortress,
fight Māra with the weapon of wisdom,
guard your success, and do not be attached.

41 Before long has passed by, alas, this body will lie on the ground,
rejected, without consciousness, just like a useless piece of wood.

42 Whatever an aggressor might do to an aggressor,
or an enemy to an enemy—
a mind that is badly-directed can do far worse than that to him.

43 Mother and father might not do for him, or other relatives,
as much good as a mind that is well-directed can do for him.

The Chapter about the Mind, the Third

4
Pupphavaggo

44 Kŏ imaṁ paṭhaviṁ vicessati
yamalokañ-ca imaṁ sadevakaṁ?
Ko dhammapadaṁ sudesitaṁ
kusalo puppham-ivappacessati?

45 Sekho paṭhaviṁ vicessati
yamalokañ-ca imaṁ sadevakaṁ.
Sekho dhammapadaṁ sudesitaṁ
kusalo puppham-ivappacessati.

46 Pheṇūpamaṁ kāyam-imaṁ viditvā,
marīcidhammaṁ abhisambudhāno,
chetvāna Mārassa papupphakāni,
adassanaṁ Maccurājassa gacche.

47 Pupphāni heva pacinantaṁ byāsattamanasaṁ naraṁ,
suttaṁ gāmaṁ mahogho va, maccu ādāya gacchati.

48 Pupphāni heva pacinantaṁ byāsattamanasaṁ naraṁ,
atittaṁ yeva kāmesu Antako kurute vasaṁ.

4

The Chapter about Flowers

44 Who will know this earth
and the lower realm, together with the gods?
Who (will reflect) on the well-taught verse of the Dharma
as a good man reflects on a flower?

45 The trainee will know this earth
and the lower realm, together with the gods.
The trainee (will reflect) on the well-taught verse of the Dharma
as a good man reflects on a flower.

46 Knowing that this body is just like froth,
understanding it has the nature of a mirage,
cutting off Māra's flower-tipped (arrows),
one should go beyond the King of Death's sight.

47 ° Death takes up and carries away the one
whose mind is attached to collecting flowers,
like a great flood (carries off) a sleeping village.

48 ° The End-Maker takes control of the one
whose mind is attached to collecting flowers,
even though he is unsated with sense pleasures.

49 Yathā pi bhamaro pupphaṁ vaṇṇagandhaṁ aheṭhayaṁ
paḷeti rasam-ādāya, evaṁ gāme munī care.

50 Na paresaṁ vilomāni, na paresaṁ katākataṁ
attano va avekkheyya, katāni akatāni ca.

51 Yathā pi ruciraṁ pupphaṁ vaṇṇavantaṁ agandhakaṁ,
evaṁ subhāsitā vācā aphalā hoti akubbato.

52 Yathā pi ruciraṁ pupphaṁ vaṇṇavantaṁ sagandhakaṁ,
evaṁ subhāsitā vācā saphalā hoti pakubbato.

53 Yathā pi puppharāsimhā kayirā mālāguṇe bahū,
evaṁ jātena maccena kattabbaṁ kusalaṁ bahuṁ.

54 Na pupphagandho paṭivātam-eti,
na candanaṁ tagaramallikā vā,
satañ-ca gandho paṭivātam-eti,
sabbā disā sappuriso pavāyati.

55 Candanaṁ tagaraṁ vā pi, uppalaṁ atha vassikī,
etesaṁ gandhajātānaṁ sīlagandho anuttaro.

56 Appamatto ayaṁ gandho yāyaṁ tagaracandanī,
yo ca sīlavataṁ gandho vāti devesu uttamo.

57 Tesaṁ sampannasīlānaṁ, appamādavihārinaṁ,
sammad-aññāvimuttānaṁ, Māro maggaṁ na vindati.

49 Just as a bee, without hurting the flower, its colour, or scent,
gathers its nectar and escapes, so should the seer roam in the village.

50 Not the wrongs of others, or what others have done or have not done
one should consider, but what has been done
and not done by oneself.

51 Just like a beautiful flower, which has colour, but lacks fragrance,
so are well-spoken words fruitless for the one who acts not (on them).

52 Just like a beautiful flower, which has colour, and has fragrance,
so are well-spoken words fruitful for the one who does act (on them).

53 Just as from a heap of flowers one might make a lot of garlands,
so should many good deeds be done by one who is born a mortal.

54 The fragrance of flowers goes not against the wind,
nor does sandalwood or pinwheel or white jasmine,
but the fragrance of the good goes against the wind,
the true person's (fragrance) permeates all directions.

55 Sandalwood, pinwheel, then water lily and striped jasmine,
amongst these kinds of fragrance virtue's fragrance is unsurpassed.

56 Pinwheel and sandalwood fragrance are insignificant,
but the fragrance of one who has virtue flutters supreme
amongst the gods.

57 ° Māra cannot find the path of those endowed with virtue,
who live heedfully,
and who are freed through complete and deep knowledge.

58 Yathā saṅkāradhānasmiṁ ujjhitasmiṁ mahāpathe
padumaṁ tattha jāyetha, sucigandhaṁ manoramaṁ,

59 evaṁ saṅkārabhūtesu, andhabhūte puthujjane,
atirocati paññāya Sammāsambuddhasāvako.

Pupphavaggo Catuttho

58⌝ Just as in a forsaken and discarded heap along the highway
a lotus might arise in that place, with a pure fragrance,
delighting the mind,

59⌟ ° so amongst the forsaken, the Perfect Sambuddha's disciple
outshines the blind and ordinary folk through his wisdom.

The Chapter about Flowers, the Fourth

5

Bālavaggo

60 Dīghā jāgarato ratti, dīghaṁ santassa yojanaṁ,
dīgho bālānaṁ saṁsāro Saddhammaṁ avijānataṁ.

61 Carañ-ce nādhigaccheyya seyyaṁ sadisam-attano,
ekacariyaṁ daḷhaṁ kayirā: natthi bāle sahāyatā.

62 "Puttā matthi, dhanam-matthi," iti bālo vihaññati,
attā hi attano natthi, kuto puttā, kuto dhanaṁ?

63 Yo bālo maññati bālyaṁ, paṇḍito vāpi tena so,
bālo ca paṇḍitamānī, sa ve bālo ti vuccati.

64 Yāvajīvam-pi ce bālo paṇḍitaṁ payirupāsati,
na so Dhammaṁ vijānāti, dabbī sūparasaṁ yathā.

65 Muhuttam-api ce viññū paṇḍitaṁ payirupāsati,
khippaṁ Dhammaṁ vijānāti, jivhā sūparasaṁ yathā.

66 Caranti bālā dummedhā amitteneva attanā,
karontā pāpakaṁ kammaṁ, yaṁ hoti kaṭukapphalaṁ.

5
The Chapter about Fools

60 Long is the night for one awake, long is a league for one tired,
long is the round of births and deaths for fools who know not
the True Dharma.

61 If while roaming one cannot find one better or the same as oneself,
one should resolve to go alone: there is no friendship with fools.

62 "Sons are mine, riches are mine," so the fool suffers vexation,
when even self is not his own, how then sons, how then riches?

63 The fool who knows (his) foolishness, is at least wise in that (matter),
the fool who is proud of his wisdom, he is said to be a fool indeed.

64 Even if a fool attends on a wise man for his whole life long,
he does not learn the Dharma,
just as spoon learns not the taste of curry.

65 If a perceptive man attends on a wise man even for a second,
he quickly learns the Dharma,
just as the tongue (learns) the taste of curry.

66 Stupid fools live having themselves as their own foes,
committing wicked deeds, which produce bitter fruit.

67 Na taṁ kammaṁ kataṁ sādhu, yaṁ katvā anutappati,
yassa assumukho rodaṁ, vipākaṁ paṭisevati.

68 Tañ-ca kammaṁ kataṁ sādhu, yaṁ katvā nānutappati,
yassa patīto sumano, vipākaṁ paṭisevati.

69 Madhuvā maññati bālo, yāva pāpaṁ na paccati,
yadā ca paccati pāpaṁ, bālo dukkhaṁ nigacchati.

70 Māse māse kusaggena bālo bhuñjetha bhojanaṁ,
na so saṅkhātadhammānaṁ kalaṁ agghati soḷasiṁ.

71 Na hi pāpaṁ kataṁ kammaṁ, sajju khīraṁ va muccati,
ḍahantaṁ bālam-anveti, bhasmacchanno va pāvako.

72 Yāvad-eva anatthāya ñattaṁ bālassa jāyati,
hanti bālassa sukkaṁsaṁ, muddham-assa vipātayaṁ.

73⌉ Asataṁ bhāvanam-iccheyya, purekkhārañ-ca bhikkhusu,
āvāsesu ca issariyaṁ, pūjā parakulesu ca:

74⌋ "Mameva kata' maññantu gihī pabbajitā ubho,
mameva ativasā assu, kiccākiccesu kismici",
iti bālassa saṅkappo, icchā māno ca vaḍḍhati.

67 That deed is not well done, which, having done, one has regret,
for which he has tears on his face, as the result follows him round.

68 But that deed is well done, which, having done, one has no regret,
for which he is pleased and happy, as the result follows him round.

69 The fool thinks it sweet, as long as the wicked deed does not ripen,
but when the wicked deed ripens, the fool undergoes suffering.

70 From month to month the fool may eat food with the tip of kusha grass,
(but) he is not worth a sixteenth part of those who have mastered the Dharma.

71 A wicked deed that has been done, like milk, does not turn all at once,
smouldering, it follows the fool, like a fire covered with ashes.

72 As far as learning arises for a fool, it is only to his disadvantage,
it destroys the fool's good fortune, and it will destroy his head.

73⌉ He may wish for the respect that is lacking, and status amongst the monastics,
for control in the living quarters, and worship amongst good families:

74⌋ "Householders and renunciants should both think this was done by me,
let them (all) be under my sway, in all to be done and not done",
so does the fool think, (meanwhile) his desires and conceit increase.

75 Aññā hi lābhūpanisā, aññā Nibbānagāminī,
evam-etaṁ abhiññāya bhikkhu Buddhassa sāvako
sakkāraṁ nābhinandeyya, vivekam-anubrūhaye.

Bālavaggo Pañcamo

75 For the means to gains is one thing,
the (path) going to Nirvāṇa another,
thus knowing this the monastic disciple of the Buddha
should not delight in honours, (but) practise in solitude.

The Chapter about Fools, the Fifth

6

Paṇḍitavaggo

76 Nidhīnaṁ va pavattāraṁ yaṁ passe vajjadassinaṁ,
niggayhavādiṁ medhāviṁ tādisaṁ paṇḍitaṁ bhaje;
tādisaṁ bhajamānassa seyyo hoti na pāpiyo.

77 Ovadeyyānusāseyya, asabbhā ca nivāraye,
sataṁ hi so piyo hoti, asataṁ hoti appiyo.

78 Na bhaje pāpake mitte, na bhaje purisādhame,
bhajetha mitte kalyāṇe, bhajetha purisuttame.

79 Dhammapīti sukhaṁ seti, vippasannena cetasā,
Ariyappavedite Dhamme sadā ramati paṇḍito.

80 Udakaṁ hi nayanti nettikā,
usukārā namayanti tejanaṁ,
dāruṁ namayanti tacchakā,
attānaṁ damayanti paṇḍitā.

81 Selo yathā ekaghano vātena na samīrati,
evaṁ nindāpasaṁsāsu na samiñjanti paṇḍitā.

6

The Chapter about the Wise

76 One should regard someone who shows your faults just like one
who points out hidden treasure,
one should keep company with such a sagacious, learned person
who reproves you;
keeping company with such is (surely) better for you, not worse.

77 One should advise and instruct, and forbid whatever is vile,
for he is dear to the good, (but) he is not dear to the bad.

78 One should not keep company with wicked friends,
one should not keep company with the ignoble,
you should keep company with spiritual friends,
you should keep company with superior people.

79 The one who drinks the Dharma lives well, with a clear mind,
the wise one will always delight in the Dharma that is made known
by the Noble.

80 Course-makers lead water,
fletchers straighten arrows,
carpenters straighten wood,
the wise master themselves.

81 Just as solid rock is not shaken by the wind,
so the wise are not moved by blame or praise.

82 Yathā pi ra̯hado gambhīro vippasanno anāvilo,
evaṁ Dhammāni sutvāna vippasīdanti paṇḍitā.

83 Sabbattha ve sappurisā cajanti,
na kāmakāmā lapayanti santo;
sukhena phuṭṭhā atha vā dukhena,
noccāvacaṁ paṇḍitā dassayanti.

84 Na attahetu na parassa hetu,
na puttam-icche na dhanaṁ na raṭṭhaṁ—
na iccheyya adhammena samiddhim-attano;
sa sīlavā paññavā dhammiko siyā.

85⌉ Appakā te manussesu ye janā pāragāmino,
athāyaṁ itarā pajā tīram-evānudhāvati,

86⌋ ye ca kho sammad-akkhāte Dhamme dhammānuvattino,
te janā pāram-essanti, maccudheyyaṁ suduttaraṁ.

87 Kaṇhaṁ dhammaṁ vippahāya, sukkaṁ bhāvetha paṇḍito,
okā anokaṁ āgamma; viveke yattha dūramaṁ,

88 Tatrābhiratim-iccheyya, hitvā kāme akiñcano,
pari̯yodapeyya attānaṁ cittaklesehi paṇḍito.

82 Like a lake that is deep, clear, and unruffled,
just so the wise are confident after listening to the Dharma.

83 True people surely everywhere renounce,
the good do not talk of desiring sense-pleasures;
when touched by pleasure or by suffering,
the wise show neither elation or depression.

84 Not for one's own sake and not for another's sake,
not desiring a child, riches, or a kingdom—
he should not desire his success through corruption;
he should be virtuous and wise and righteous.

85⌝ Amongst humans few people go beyond,
the rest of the people run down the bank,

86⌟ but those who live righteously,
conforming with this well-taught Dharma,
those folk will go beyond the realm of death,
which is very hard to cross.

87 Having abandoned the dark state,
the wise one should develop the bright,
having gone forth to homelessness from home;
in solitude, where it is hard to delight.

88 One should desire to delight in that place,
having given up sense pleasures, and having no possessions,
the wise one should purify the self of defilements of mind.

89 Yesaṁ sambodhi-aṅgesu sammā cittaṁ subhāvitaṁ,
ādānapaṭinissagge anupādāya ye ratā,
khīṇāsavā jutimanto, te loke parinibbutā.

Paṇḍitavaggo Chaṭṭho

89 For those who have well developed with right mind the factors of complete awakening,
having given up grasping, those who delight in being unattached,
pollutant-free, shining forth, are emancipated in the world.

The Chapter about the Wise, the Sixth

7

Arahantavaggo

90 Gataddhino visokassa vippamuttassa sabbadhi,
sabbaganthappahīnassa, pariḷāho na vijjati.

91 Uyyuñjanti satīmanto na nikete ramanti te,
haṁsā va pallalaṁ hitvā, okam-okaṁ jahanti te.

92 Yesaṁ sannicayo natthi, ye pariññātabhojanā,
suññato animitto ca vimokkho yesa' gocaro,
ākāse va sakuntānaṁ, gati tesaṁ durannayā

93 Yassāsavā parikkhīṇā, āhāre ca anissito,
suññato animitto ca vimokkho yassa gocaro,
ākāse va sakuntānaṁ, padaṁ tassa durannayaṁ.

94 Yassindriyāni samathaṁ gatāni,
assā yathā sārathinā sudantā,
pahīnamānassa anāsavassa—
devā pi tassa pihayanti tādino.

95 Paṭhavisamo no virujjhati,
indakhīlūpamŏ tādi subbato,
rahado va apetakaddamo—
saṁsārā na bhavanti tādino.

7
The Chapter about the Arhats

90 For the one who has reached his goal, who grieves not,
 being released on all sides,
who has abandoned all the knots, no consuming fever is found.

91 The mindful ones who are striving do not delight in a dwelling,
like geese who abandon a lake, they abandon fondness for homes.

92 For those who have no stores, those who comprehend food aright,
for those whose resort is the liberation that is empty or signless,
like the birds in the sky, their track is hard to find.

93 For him whose pollutants are destroyed,
 who is not dependent on the foods,
for him whose resort is the liberation that is empty or signless,
like the birds in the sky, his footprint is hard to find.

94 For the one whose senses are stilled,
like horses well-trained by their charioteer,
who has abandoned conceit, who is without pollutants—
even the gods envy such a one.

95 One untroubled just like the earth,
steadfast just like a city-post,
like a lake mud-free—
such a one continues not in births and deaths.

96 Santaṁ tassa manaṁ hoti, santā vācā ca kamma' ca,
sammad-aññāvimuttassa, upasantassa tādino.

97 Assaddho akataññū ca sandhicchedo ca yo naro,
hatāvakāso vantāso, sa ve uttamaporiso.

98 Gāme vā yadi vāraññe, ninne vā yadi vā thale,
yattharahanto viharanti, taṁ bhūmiṁ rāmaṇeyyakaṁ.

99 Ramaṇīyāni araññāni yattha na ramatī jano,
vītarāgā ramissanti, na te kāmagavesino.

Arahantavaggo Sattamo

96 His mind is calm, his speech and his actions are also calm,
liberated by right knowledge, such a one is (truly) peaceful.

97 The person who is beyond (mere) faith, who knows that
which is unmade, who has cut off (rebirth-)linking,
who has destroyed the occasion, who has thrown out
hope and desire, is surely the person supreme.

98 Whether in the village or wilds, whether on low or on high ground,
wherever the Arhats live, that ground is (surely) delightful.

99 The delightful wildernesses where the people do not delight,
those without passion will take delight,
(but) not those who seek sense pleasures.

The Chapter about Arhats, the Seventh

8

Sahassavaggo

100 Sahassam-api ce vācā anatthapadasaṁhitā,
ekaṁ atthapadaṁ seyyo yaṁ sutvā upasammati.

101 Sahassam-api ce gāthā anatthapadasaṁhitā,
ekaṁ gāthāpadaṁ seyyo yaṁ sutvā upasammati.

102 Yo ce gāthāsataṁ bhāse anatthapadasaṁhitā,
ekaṁ Dhammapadaṁ seyyo, yaṁ sutvā upasammati.

103 Yo sahassaṁ sahassena saṅgāme mānuse jine,
ekañ-ca jeyya attānaṁ, sa ve saṅgāmajuttamo.

104⌉ Attā have jitaṁ seyyo yā cāyaṁ itarā pajā,
attadantassa posassa, niccaṁ saññatacārino,

105⌋ neva devo na gandhabbo, na Māro saha Brahmunā,
jitaṁ apajitaṁ kayirā tathārūpassa jantuno.

8
The Chapter about the Thousands

100 Though there are a thousand sayings consisting of useless words,
better is one useful word hearing which one is brought to peace.

101 Though there are a thousand verses consisting of useless words,
better is one word of a verse hearing which one is brought
to peace.

102 One may speak a thousand verses consisting of useless words,
better is one verse of the Dharma, hearing which one is brought
to peace.

103 One may conquer a thousand men a thousand times in a battle,
but having conquered one's own self,
one would surely be supreme in battle.

104⌉ Conquest over self is better than that over other people,
for the person who conquers himself,
who lives constantly well-restrained,

105⌋ neither gods, nor gandharvas, nor Māra together with Brahmās,
can turn conquest into defeat for a person who is like this.

106 Māse māse sahassena yo yajetha sataṁ samaṁ;
ekañ-ca bhāvitattānaṁ muhuttam-api pūjaye—
sā yeva pūjanā seyyo yañ-ce vassasataṁ hutaṁ.

107 Yo ca vassasataṁ jantu aggiṁ paricare vane;
ekañ-ca bhāvitattānaṁ muhuttam-api pūjaye—
sā yeva pūjanā seyyo yañ-ce vassasataṁ hutaṁ.

108 Yaṁ kiñci yiṭṭhaṁ ca hutaṁ ca loke
saṁvaccharaṁ yajetha puññapekkho,
sabbam-pi taṁ na catubhāgam-eti—
abhivādanā ujjugatesu seyyo.

109 Abhivādanasīlissa niccaṁ vaddhāpacāyino,
cattāro dhammā vaḍḍhanti: āyu vaṇṇo sukhaṁ balaṁ.

110 Yo ca vassasataṁ jīve, dussīlo asamāhito,
ekāhaṁ jīvitaṁ seyyo, sīlavantassa jhāyino.

111 Yo ca vassasataṁ jīve, duppañño asamāhito,
ekāhaṁ jīvitaṁ seyyo, paññavantassa jhāyino.

112 Yo ca vassasataṁ jīve, kusīto hīnavīriyo,
ekāhaṁ jīvitaṁ seyyo, viriyam-ārabhato daḷhaṁ.

113 Yo ca vassasataṁ jīve apassaṁ udayabbayaṁ,
ekāhaṁ jīvitaṁ seyyo passato udayabbayaṁ.

106 One might give alms impartially with a thousand (coins of money)
month by month for a hundred (years);
and one might worship someone with developed self for a second—
that worship is surely better than the hundred-year sacrifice.

107 One person might care for the fire in the woods for a hundred years;
and one might worship someone with developed self for a second—
that worship is surely better than the hundred-year sacrifice.

108 Whatever the alms or the sacrifice in the world
the one seeking merit may give for a year,
all that comes not to a quarter (of the merit)—
better is the worship of the upright.

109 For the one who is constantly worshipping honourable elders,
four things increase: the length of life, beauty, happiness,
and strength.

110 One might live for a hundred years, unvirtuous and uncomposed,
(but) a life of one day is better, for one with virtue and meditation.

111 One might live for a hundred years,
lacking in wisdom and uncomposed,
(but) a life of one day is better, for one endowed with wisdom
and meditation.

112 One might live for a hundred years, indolent, with less energy,
(but) a life of one day is better, for one with energy set up and firm.

113 One might live for a hundred years without seeing rise and fall,
(but) a life of one day is better (for the one) seeing rise and fall.

114 Yo ca vassasataṁ jīve apassaṁ amataṁ padaṁ,
ekāhaṁ jīvitaṁ seyyo passato amataṁ padaṁ.

115 Yo ca vassasataṁ jīve apassaṁ dhammam-uttamaṁ,
ekāhaṁ jīvitaṁ seyyo passato dhammam-uttamaṁ.

Sahassavaggo Aṭṭhamo

114 One might live for a hundred years without seeing the deathless state,
(but) a life of one day is better (for one) seeing the deathless state.

115 One might live for a hundred years without seeing the supreme state,
(but) a life of one day is better (for one) seeing the supreme state.

The Chapter about the Thousands, the Eighth

9

Pāpavaggo

116 Abhittharetha kalyāṇe, pāpā cittaṁ nivāraye,
dandhaṁ hi karato puññaṁ pāpasmiṁ ramatī mano.

117 Pāpañ-ce puriso kayi̭rā, na taṁ kayi̭rā punappunaṁ,
na tamhi chandaṁ kayi̭rātha, dukkho pāpassa uccayo.

118 Puññañ-ce puriso kayi̭rā, kayi̭rāthetaṁ punappunaṁ,
tamhi chandaṁ kayirātha, sukho puññassa uccayo.

119 Pāpo pi passati bhadraṁ yāva pāpaṁ na paccati,
yadā ca paccati pāpaṁ atha pāpo pāpāni passati.

120 Bhadro pi passati pāpaṁ yāva bhadraṁ na paccati,
yadā ca paccati bhadraṁ atha bhadro bhadrāni passati.

9
The Chapter about Wickedness

116 Hasten to do wholesome deeds, ward off the mind from wickedness,
for the mind of the one slow in merit delights in wickedness.

117 Should a person do that which is wicked,
he should not do it again and again,
let him not place his intention in it, (for) there is an accumulation
of suffering for the wicked one.

118 If a person should make merit, he should do it again and again,
let him place his intention there, there is an increase of joy
or the one who has made merit.

119 Even the wicked one experiences good fortune while the
wickedness does not ripen,
but when the wickedness ripens then the wicked one experiences
wicked things.

120 Even the fortunate one experiences wickedness
as long as the good fortune does not ripen,
but when the fortune ripens then the fortunate one experiences
good fortune.

121 Māppamaññetha pāpassa: na maṁ taṁ āgamissati,
udabindunipātena udakumbho pi pūrati,
bālo pūrati pāpassa, thokaṁ thokam-pi ācinaṁ.

122 Māppamaññetha puññassa: na maṁ taṁ āgamissati.
udabindunipātena udakumbho pi pūrati,
dhīro pūrati puññassa, thokathokam-pi ācinaṁ.

123 Vāṇijo va bhayaṁ maggaṁ, appasattho mahaddhano,
visaṁ jīvitukāmo va, pāpāni parivajjaye.

124 Pāṇimhi ce vaṇo nāssa hareyya pāṇinā visaṁ,
nābbaṇaṁ visam-anveti, natthi pāpaṁ akubbato.

125 So appaduṭṭhassa narassa dussati,
suddhassa posassa anaṅgaṇassa,
tam-eva bālaṁ pacceti pāpaṁ,
sukhumo rajo paṭivātaṁ va khitto.

126 Gabbham-eke 'papajjanti, nirayaṁ pāpakammino,
saggaṁ sugatino yanti, parinibbanti anāsavā.

127 Na antalikkhe, na samuddamajjhe,
na pabbatānaṁ vivaraṁ pavissa:
na vijjatī so jagatippadeso
yatthaṭṭhito mucceyya pāpakammā.

121 One should not despise a wickedness (thinking):
it will not come to me,
through the falling of water drops the water-pot is (quickly) filled,
the fool, gathering bit by bit, becomes full of wickedness.

122 One should not despise merit (thinking): it will not come to me,
through the falling of water drops the water-pot is (quickly) filled,
the wise one, gathering bit by bit, becomes full of merit.

123 Like a merchant on a fearful path, with few friends and great wealth,
as one loving life (would avoid) poison,
(so) should one avoid wicked deeds.

124 If there is no wound in his hand he can carry poison with his hand,
poison does not enter without a wound,
there is no bad result for the one who does no (wrong).

125 One offends against the inoffensive one,
a purified and passionless person,
that wicked deed (then) returns to the fool,
like fine dust that is thrown against the wind.

126 Some are reborn in the womb,
(but) those who are wicked in the underworld,
the righteous go to heaven,
those who are pollutant-free are emancipated.

127 Neither in the sky, nor in the middle of the ocean,
nor after entering a mountain cleft:
there is no place found on this earth
where one can be free from (the results of) wicked deeds.

128 Na antalikkhe, na samuddamajjhe,
na pabbatānaṁ vivaraṁ pavissa:
na vijjatī so jagatippadeso,
yatthaṭṭhitaṁ nappasahetha maccu.

Pāpavaggo Navamo

128 Neither in the sky, nor in the middle of the ocean,
nor after entering a mountain cleft:
there is no place found on this earth,
in which death does not overcome one.

The Chapter about Wickedness, the Ninth

10

Daṇḍavaggo

129 Sabbe tasanti daṇḍassa, sabbe bhāyanti maccuno,
attānaṁ upamaṁ katvā, na haneyya na ghātaye.

130 Sabbe tasanti daṇḍassa, sabbesaṁ jīvitaṁ piyaṁ,
attānaṁ upamaṁ katvā, na haneyya na ghātaye.

131 Sukhakāmāni bhūtāni yo daṇḍena vihiṁsati,
attano sukham-esāno, pecca so na labhate sukhaṁ.

132 Sukhakāmāni bhūtāni yo daṇḍena na hiṁsati,
attano sukham-esāno, pecca so labhate sukhaṁ.

133 Māvoca pharusaṁ kañci, vuttā paṭivadeyyu' taṁ,
dukkhā hi sārambhakathā, paṭidaṇḍā phuseyyu' taṁ.

134 Sace neresi attānaṁ kaṁso upahato yathā,
esa pattosi Nibbānaṁ, sārambho te na vijjati.

10
The Chapter about the Stick

129 Everyone trembles at the stick, everyone is in fear of death,
comparing oneself (with others),
one should not hurt or have (them) hurt.

130 Everyone trembles at the stick, for all of them life is dear,
comparing oneself (with others),
one should not hurt or have (them) hurt.

131 One who harms with a stick beings who desire happiness,
while seeking happiness for himself,
won't find happiness after death.

132 One who harms not with a stick beings who desire happiness,
while seeking happiness for himself, will find happiness after death.

133 Do not say anything harsh,
spoken to they might answer back to you,
for arrogant talk entails misery,
and they might strike you back with a stick.

134 If you make no sound like a gong that is broken,
you are (like) one who has attained Nirvāṇa,
contention is not found in you.

135 Yathā daṇḍena gopālo gāvo pāceti gocaraṁ,
evaṁ jarā ca maccu ca āyuṁ pācenti pāṇinaṁ.

136 Atha pāpāni kammāni karaṁ bālo na bujjhati,
sehi kammehi dummedho aggidaḍḍho va tappati.

137⌝ Yo daṇḍena adaṇḍesu appaduṭṭhesu dussati
dasannam-aññataraṁ ṭhānaṁ khippam-eva nigacchati:

138 vedanaṁ pharusaṁ, jāniṁ, sarīrassa ca bhedanaṁ,
garukaṁ vā pi ābādhaṁ, cittakkhepaṁ va pāpuṇe,

139 rājato vā upassaggaṁ, abbhakkhānaṁ va dāruṇaṁ,
parikkhayaṁ va ñātīnaṁ, bhogānaṁ va pabhaṅguraṁ,

140⌟ atha vāssa agārāni aggi ḍahati pāvako,
kāyassa bhedā duppañño nirayaṁ so upapajjati.

141 Na naggacariyā na jaṭā na paṅkā,
nānāsakā thaṇḍilasāyikā vā,
rājo ca jallaṁ ukkuṭikappadhānaṁ,
sodhenti maccaṁ avitiṇṇakaṅkhaṁ.

142 Alaṅkato ce pi samaṁ careyya,
santo danto niyato brahmacārī,
sabbesu bhūtesu nidhāya daṇḍaṁ,
so brāhmaṇo so samaṇo sa bhikkhu.

143 Hirīnisedho puriso koci lokasmi' vijjati,
yo nindaṁ appabodhati, asso bhadro kasām-iva.

135 Like a cowherd with a stick drives cattle to pasture,
so do old age and death drive life out of beings.

136 The fool does not understand the wicked deeds he is doing,
the stupid one is consumed by his deeds as (by) a burning fire.

137⌉ Whoever offends with a stick those who are inoffensive and harmless
will quickly fall into one of ten states:

138 harsh feelings, loss (of his wealth), and the break up of the body,
or even heavy affliction, or surely he will lose his mind,

139 (there may be) danger from the King, or slander that is terrible,
(he may suffer from) loss of kin, or (from) the destruction of wealth,

140⌋ also his houses may be consumed by flames and fire,
and at the break-up of the body that one lacking in wisdom
will arise in the underworld.

141 Not going naked, nor matted hair, nor mud,
nor fasting or lying on stony ground,
dust and dirt, (or) striving while squatting,
can purify a mortal who has not removed uncertainty.

142 Even if he were to adorn himself,
(but) is peaceful, trained, settled, spiritual,
and has put aside the stick towards all beings,
he is a brahmin, an ascetic, a monastic.

143 Whatever person in the world is found restrained by conscience,
and is aware of his fault, is like a good horse that is (restrained)
by a whip.

144 Asso yathā bhadro kasāniviṭṭho,
ātāpino saṁvegino bhavātha.
Saddhāya sīlena ca vīriyena ca,
samādhinā Dhammavinicchayena ca.
Sampannavijjācaraṇā patissatā,
pahassatha dukkham-idaṁ anappakaṁ.

145 Udakaṁ hi nayanti nettikā,
usukārā namayanti tejanaṁ,
dāruṁ namayanti tacchakā,
attānaṁ damayanti subbatā.

Daṇḍavaggo Dasamo

144 Like a good horse restrained by the whip,
you should be ardent and spiritually intense.
Having faith, virtue, and energy,
concentration and investigation of the Dharma.
One who has understanding and good conduct, mindfulness,
will abandon this not insignificant suffering.

145 Course-makers lead water,
fletchers straighten arrows,
carpenters straighten wood,
the mild master themselves.

The Chapter about the Stick, the Tenth

11

Jarāvaggo

146 Ko nu hāso, kim-ānando, niccaṁ pajjalite sati,
andhakārena onaddhā, padīpaṁ na gavesatha?

147 Passa cittakataṁ bimbaṁ, arukāyaṁ samussitaṁ,
āturaṁ bahusaṅkappaṁ, yassa natthi dhuvaṁ ṭhiti.

148 Parijiṇṇam-idaṁ rūpaṁ, roganīḷaṁ pabhaṅguraṁ,
bhijjati pūtisandeho, maraṇantaṁ hi jīvitaṁ.

149 Yānimāni apatthāni alāpūneva sārade
kāpotakāni aṭṭhīni, tāni disvāna kā rati?

150 Aṭṭhīnaṁ nagaraṁ kataṁ,
maṁsalohitalepanaṁ,
yattha jarā ca maccu ca,
māno makkho ca ohito.

151 Jīranti ve rājarathā sucittā,
atho sarīram-pi jaraṁ upeti,
satañ-ca Dhammo na jaraṁ upeti,
santo have sabbhi pavedayanti.

11
The Chapter about Old Age

146 Why this laughter, why this joy,
when the world is constantly burning,
why, when enveloped by darkness, do you not seek for a light?

147 See this beautified manikin, a heap of sores that is raised up,
sick, imagined in many ways, which has nothing stable or firm.

148 This body is worn out, a nest of disease, perishing,
the putrid body comes to destruction, for life ends in death.

149 Like discarded white gourds thrown away in autumn
are these grey bones; seeing them, why is there delight?

150 This fortress is made out of bones,
plastered over with flesh and blood,
but hidden within lie old age,
death, also conceit and anger.

151 Decorated royal chariots decay,
and the body also decays,
but the good Dharma does not decay,
the good surely pass it on to the good.

152 Appassutāyaṁ puriso balivaddo va jīrati,
maṁsāni tassa vaḍḍhanti, paññā tassa na vaḍḍhati.

153 Anekajātisaṁsāraṁ sandhāvissaṁ anibbisaṁ
gahakārakaṁ gavesanto: dukkhā jāti punappunaṁ.

154 Gahakāraka diṭṭhosi! Puna gehaṁ na kāhasi:
sabbā te phāsukā bhaggā, gahakūṭaṁ visaṅkhitaṁ,
visaṅkhāragataṁ cittaṁ, taṇhānaṁ khayam-ajjhagā.

155 Acaritvā brahmacariyaṁ, aladdhā yobbane dhanaṁ,
jiṇṇakoñcā ca jhāyanti khīṇamacche va pallale.

156 Acaritvā brahmacariyaṁ aladdhā yobbane dhanaṁ
senti cāpātikhittā va, purāṇāni anutthunaṁ.

Jarāvaggo Ekādasamo

152 The person of little learning increases in age like an ox,
(for although) his flesh does increase, his wisdom does not increase.

153⌉ Through the round of countless births and deaths I have wandered
without finding
the housebuilder I was seeking: born and suffering once again.

154⌋ O housebuilder, now you are seen!
You will not build the house again:
all your rafters have been broken,
and the ridgepole has been destroyed,
my mind has reached the unconditioned,
and craving's end has been achieved.

155 Not having lived the holy life,
not having gained wealth in their youth,
they waste away like herons in a small lake devoid of fish.

156 Not having lived the holy life,
not having gained wealth in their youth,
they lie like (shafts) shot from a bow, wailing about things in the past.

The Chapter about Old Age, the Eleventh

12

Attavaggo

157 Attānañ-ce piyaṁ jaññā rakkheyya naṁ surakkhitaṁ,
tiṇṇam-aññataraṁ yāmaṁ paṭijaggeyya paṇḍito.

158 Attānam-eva paṭhamaṁ patirūpe nivesaye,
athaññam-anusāseyya, na kilisseyya paṇḍito.

159 Attānañ-ce tathā kayirā yathaññam-anusāsati,
sudanto vata dametha, attā hi kira duddamo.

160 Attā hi attano nātho, ko hi nātho paro siyā?
Attanā va sudantena nāthaṁ labhati dullabhaṁ.

161 Attanā va kataṁ pāpaṁ, attajaṁ attasambhavaṁ,
abhimatthati dummedhaṁ vajiraṁ vasmamayaṁ maṇiṁ.

162. Yassa accantadussīlyaṁ māluvā Sālam-ivotataṁ
karoti so tathattānaṁ yathā naṁ icchatī diso.

12

The Chapter about the Self

157 If one regards oneself as dear one should guard oneself right well,
during one of the three watches (of the night)
the wise one should stay alert.

158 First one should establish oneself in what is suitable,
then one can advise another,
the wise one should not have (any) defilement.

159 He should do himself as he would advise another (to do),
being well-trained, he could surely train (another),
for it is said the self is difficult to train.

160 For the self is the friend of self, for what other friend would there be?
When the self is well-trained, one finds a friend that is hard to find.

161 That wickedness done by oneself, born in oneself, arising in oneself,
crushes the one who is stupid, as a diamond (crushes) a rock-jewel.

162 The one who is covered with an exceeding lack of virtue,
like a deadly creeper on a Sal tree,
makes himself the same as his enemy wishes him to be.

163 Sukarāni asādhūni, attano ahitāni ca,
yaṁ ve hitañ-ca sādhuñ-ca taṁ ve paramadukkaraṁ.

164 Yo sāsanaṁ arahataṁ Ariyānaṁ Dhammajīvinaṁ
paṭikkosati dummedho diṭṭhiṁ nissāya pāpikaṁ,
phalāni kaṭṭhakasseva attaghaññāya phallati.

165 Attanā va kataṁ pāpaṁ, attanā saṅkilissati,
attanā akataṁ pāpaṁ, attanā va visujjhati,
suddhī asuddhī paccattaṁ, nāñño aññaṁ visodhaye.

166 Atta-d-atthaṁ paratthena bahunā pi na hāpaye;
atta-d-attham-abhiññāya sa-d-atthapasuto siyā.

Attavaggo Dvādasamo

163 Easily done are things not good, and unbeneficial for oneself,
but that which is beneficial and good is supremely hard to do.

164 ° Whoever reviles the worthy teaching of the Noble Ones
who live by the Dharma,
that stupid one, depending on wicked views,
like the bamboo when it bears fruit, brings about his own destruction.

165 By oneself alone is a wicked deed done, by oneself is one defiled,
by oneself is a wicked deed left undone, by oneself is one purified,
purity and impurity come from oneself,
(for) no one can purify another.

166 One should not neglect one's own good for another's, however great;
knowing what is good for oneself one should be intent on that good.

The Chapter about the Self, the Twelfth

13
Lokavaggo

167 Hīnaṁ dhammaṁ na seveyya, pamādena na saṁvase,
micchādiṭṭhiṁ na seveyya, na siyā lokavaḍḍhano.

168 Uttiṭṭhe nappamajjeyya, Dhammaṁ sucaritaṁ care,
Dhammacārī sukhaṁ seti asmiṁ loke paramhi ca.

169 Dhammaṁ care sucaritaṁ, na naṁ duccaritaṁ care,
Dhammacārī sukhaṁ seti asmiṁ loke paramhi ca.

170 Yathā bubbulakaṁ passe, yathā passe marīcikaṁ,
evaṁ lokaṁ avekkhantaṁ Maccurājā na passati.

171 Etha passathimaṁ lokaṁ cittaṁ rājarathūpamaṁ,
yattha bālā visīdanti— natthi saṅgo vijānataṁ.

172 Yo ca pubbe pamajjitvā, pacchā so nappamajjati,
sŏ imaṁ lokaṁ pabhāseti abbhā mutto va candimā.

13

The Chapter about the World

167 One should not follow lowly things, one should not abide heedlessly,
one should not follow a wrong view,
one should not foster worldliness.

168 One should strive, not be heedless, one should live by the Dharma,
with good conduct,
living by the Dharma one lives at ease in this world and the next.

169 One should live by the Dharma, with good conduct,
not with bad conduct,
living by the Dharma one lives at ease in this world and the next.

170 One should see it as a bubble, one should see it as a mirage,
looking on the world in this way the King of Death does not see (one).

171 Come, look upon this world adorned like a king's gilded chariot,
where fools become depressed—
there is no bond for those who understand.

172 Whoever was heedless before, but later is not heedless,
that one shines brightly on this world
like the moon released from a cloud.

173 Yassa pāpaṁ kataṁ kammaṁ kusalena pithīyati—
sŏ imaṁ lokaṁ pabhāseti abbhā mutto va candimā.

174 Andhabhūto ayaṁ loko, tanukettha vipassati,
sakunto jālamutto va appo saggāya gacchati.

175 Haṁsādiccapathe yanti, ākāse yanti iddhiyā,
nīyanti dhīrā lokamhā, jetvā Māraṁ savāhanaṁ.

176 Ekaṁ dhammaṁ atītassa, musāvādissa jantuno,
vitiṇṇaparalokassa, natthi pāpaṁ akāriyaṁ.

177 Na ve kadar̤iyā devalokaṁ vajanti,
bālā have nappasaṁsanti dānaṁ,
dhīro ca dānaṁ anumodamāno,
teneva so hoti sukhī parattha.

178 Pathavyā ekarajjena, saggassa gamanena vā,
sabbalokādhipaccena— sotāpattiphalaṁ varaṁ.

Lokavaggo Terasamo

173 The one whose wicked deed is covered over by a good deed—
that one shines brightly on this world
like the moon released from a cloud.

174 This world is blind, few here have true insight,
as few go to heaven as birds that escape from the net.

175 Geese go through the path of the sky,
they go through the firmament by their power,
the wise are led out of the world, after beating Māra and his host.

176 For the person speaking falsely,
who has transgressed in this one thing,
who has abandoned the next world,
there is no wickedness left undone.

177 The miserly go not to the world of the gods,
fools surely do not praise giving,
but the wise one rejoices in giving,
and through that he is happy hereafter.

178 Having sole sovereignty over the earth, or going to heaven,
or lordship over the whole world—
better is the fruit of stream-entry.

The Chapter about the World, the Thirteenth

14
Buddhavaggo

179 Yassa jitaṁ nāvajīyati,
jitaṁ assa no yāti koci loke,
tam-Buddham-anantagocaraṁ,
apadaṁ kena padena nessatha?

180 Yassa jālinī visattikā,
taṇhā natthi kuhiñci netave,
tam-Buddham-anantagocaraṁ,
apadaṁ kena padena nessatha?

181 Ye jhānapasutā dhīrā, nekkhammūpasame ratā,
devā pi tesaṁ pihayanti, Sambuddhānaṁ satīmataṁ.

182 Kiccho manussapaṭilābho, kicchaṁ maccāna' jīvitaṁ,
kicchaṁ Saddhammasavanaṁ, kiccho Buddhānam-uppādo.

183 Sabbapāpassa akaraṇaṁ, kusalassa upasampadā,
sacittapariyodapanaṁ—etaṁ Buddhāna' sāsanaṁ.

14
The Chapter about the Buddha

179 He whose victory cannot be undone,
whose victory no one here approaches,
the Buddha, whose range is endless,
by what path can you lead the pathless one?

180 ° For him there is no desire, attachment,
or craving to lead (him) anywhere,
the Buddha, whose range is endless,
by what path can you lead the pathless one?

181 Those wise ones intent on meditation,
who delight in the peace of renunciation,
even the gods are envious of them, the Sambuddhas,
the ones who are mindful.

182 It is rare to acquire (birth as a) human, rare is the life of mortals,
it is rare to hear the True Dharma, rare the arising of Buddhas.

183 The non-doing of anything wicked, undertaking of what is good,
the purification of one's mind—this is the teaching of the Buddhas.

184 Khantī paramaṁ tapo titikkhā,
Nibbānaṁ paramaṁ vadanti Buddhā,
na hi pabbajito parūpaghātī,
samaṇo hoti paraṁ viheṭhayanto.

185 Anupavādo anupaghāto, pātimokkhe ca saṁvaro,
mattaññutā ca bhattasmiṁ, pantañ-ca sayanāsanaṁ,
adhicitte ca āyogo—etaṁ Buddhāna' sāsanaṁ.

186⌉ Na kahāpaṇavassena titti kāmesu vijjati,
"Appassādā dukhā kāmā," iti viññāya paṇḍito,

187⌋ api dibbesu kāmesu ratiṁ so nādhigacchati.
Taṇhakkhayarato hoti Sammāsambuddhasāvako.

188⌉ Bahuṁ ve saraṇaṁ yanti pabbatāni vanāni ca
ārāmarukkhacetyāni, manussā bhayatajjitā.

189⌋ Netaṁ kho saraṇaṁ khemaṁ, netaṁ saraṇam-uttamaṁ,
netaṁ saraṇam-āgamma sabbadukkhā pamuccati.

190⌉ Yo ca Buddhañ-ca Dhammañ-ca Saṅghañ-ca saraṇaṁ gato,
cattāri ar̤iyasaccāni sammappaññāya passati:

191 Dukkhaṁ dukkhasamuppādaṁ dukkhassa ca atikkamaṁ,
ar̤iyañ-caṭṭhaṅgikaṁ maggaṁ dukkhūpasamagāminaṁ.

192⌋ Etaṁ kho saraṇaṁ khemaṁ, etaṁ saraṇam-uttamaṁ,
etaṁ saraṇam-āgamma sabbadukkhā pamuccati.

193 Dullabho purisājañño, na so sabbattha jāyati,
yattha so jāyate dhīro, taṁ kulaṁ sukham-edhati.

184 Enduring patience is the supreme austerity,
Nirvāṇa is supreme say the Buddhas,
for one gone forth does not hurt another,
(nor does) an ascetic harass another.

185 Not finding fault, not hurting, restraint by the regulations,
knowing the right measure of food, (living in) a remote dwelling,
devotion to meditation—this is the teaching of the Buddhas.

186⌉ Not through a rain of coins is satisfaction found for sense desires,
the wise one knowing: "Sense pleasures have little joy,
(much) suffering,"

187⌋ does not find delight even in heavenly pleasures.
The disciple of the Perfect Sambuddha delights
in craving's destruction.

188⌉ ° Many people shaken by fear go for refuge
to woods and mountains, to tree shrines in pleasure parks.

189⌋ That is not a secure refuge, that is not the refuge supreme,
that is not the refuge to come to that liberates from all suffering.

190⌉ Whoever has gone for refuge to the Buddha, the Dharma,
and the Saṅgha,
and who sees with right wisdom the four noble truths:

191 Suffering, arising of suffering, and the overcoming of suffering,
the eightfold noble path leading to the stilling of suffering.

192⌋ That is a secure refuge, that is the refuge supreme,
that is the refuge to come to that liberates from all suffering.

193 A person of good breed is rare, that one is not born everywhere,
wherever that wise one is born, that family gains happiness.

194 Sukho Buddhānam-uppādo, sukhā Saddhammadesanā,
sukhā Saṅghassa sāmaggī, samaggānaṁ tapo sukho.

195⌉ Pūjārahe pūjayato, Buddhe yadi va sāvake,
papañcasamatikkante, tiṇṇasokapariddave;

196⌋ te tādise pūjayato, nibbute akutobhaye,
na sakkā puññaṁ saṅkhātuṁ, imettam-api kenaci.

Buddhavaggo Cuddasamo

194 The arising of the Buddhas is good,
the teaching of the True Dharma is good,
the harmony of the Saṅgha is good, devotion to harmony is good.

195⌉ For those who worship those worthy of worship,
whether Buddhas or disciples,
who have overcome the impediments,
crossed over grief and lamentation;

196⌋ for those who worship such as these, the emancipated, the fearless,
no one is able to measure their (vast) merit,
(saying:) it is as much as this.

The Chapter about the Buddha, the Fourteenth

15

Sukhavaggo

197 Susukhaṁ vata jīvāma verinesu averino,
verinesu manussesu viharāma averino.

198 Susukhaṁ vata jīvāma āturesu anāturā,
āturesu manussesu viharāma anāturā.

199 Susukhaṁ vata jīvāma ussukesu anussukā
ussukesu manussesu viharāma anussukā.

200 Susukhaṁ vata jīvāma yesaṁ no natthi kiñcanaṁ,
pītibhakkhā bhavissāma devā Ābhassarā yathā.

201 Jayaṁ veraṁ pasavati, dukkhaṁ seti parājito,
upasanto sukhaṁ seti, hitvā jayaparājayaṁ.

202 Natthi rāgasamo aggi, natthi dosasamo kali,
natthi khandhasamā dukkhā, natthi santiparaṁ sukhaṁ.

15

The Chapter about Happiness

197 Let us live truly happily, without hatred,
   amongst those who have hatred,
amongst humans who have hatred let us live without hatred.

198 Let us live truly happily, without sickness,
   amongst those who are sick,
amongst humans who have sickness let us live without sickness.

199 Let us live truly happily, without longing,
   amongst those who are longing,
amongst humans who are longing let us live without longing.

200 We live truly happily enough having no possessions ourselves,
we will feed on joy like the gods of Streaming Light.

201 The victor generates hatred, the defeated one finds suffering,
the one at peace lives happily,
   having abandoned victory and defeat.

202 There is no fire like passion, there is no offence like hatred,
there is no suffering like the components (of mind and body),
   no happiness other than peace.

203 Jighacchā paramā rogā, saṅkhāraparamā dukhā,
etaṁ ñatvā yathābhūtaṁ, Nibbānaṁ paramaṁ sukhaṁ.

204 Ārogyaparamā lābhā, santuṭṭhi paramaṁ dhanaṁ,
vissāsā paramā ñāti, Nibbānaṁ paramaṁ sukhaṁ.

205 Pavivekarasaṁ pitvā, rasaṁ upasamassa ca,
niddaro hoti nippāpo, Dhammapītirasaṁ pivaṁ.

206 Sāhu dassanam-ariyānaṁ, sannivāso sadā sukho,
adassanena bālānaṁ niccam-eva sukhī siyā.

207 Bālasaṅgatacārī hi dīgham-addhāna' socati,
dukkho bālehi saṁvāso amitteneva sabbadā,
dhīro ca sukhasaṁvāso ñātīnaṁ va samāgamo.

tasmā hi,
208 dhīrañ-ca paññañ-ca bahussutañ-ca,
dhorayhasīlaṁ vatavantam-ariyaṁ—
taṁ tādisaṁ sappurisaṁ sumedhaṁ
bhajetha nakkhattapathaṁ va candimā.

Sukhavaggo Paṇṇarasamo

203 Hunger is the supreme sickness,
conditions are the supreme suffering,
knowing this as it really is, (know) Nirvāṇa is the supreme good.

204 Health is the supreme gain, content the supreme wealth,
confidence the supreme kin, Nirvāṇa the supreme good.

205 Savouring the taste of solitude, and the taste of peace,
he is fearless, faultless, savouring the joyful taste of the Dharma.

206 Meeting with the noble is good,
living together (with them) is always pleasant,
through not meeting foolish people one will constantly be happy.

207 For he who consorts with fools grieves for a long time,
dwelling with fools is always suffering as it is with enemies,
the wise one dwells happily as with an assembly of kin.

therefore,
208 the firm, the wise, and the learned,
the virtuous, dutiful, and noble—
° (accompany) such a true and intelligent person
as the moon accompanies the course of the stars.

The Chapter about Happiness, the Fifteenth

16

Piyavaggo

209 Ayoge yuñjam-attānaṁ, yogasmiñ-ca ayojayaṁ,
atthaṁ hitvā piyaggāhī, pihetattānuyoginaṁ.

210 Mā piyehi samāgañchī appiyehi kudācanaṁ,
piyānaṁ adassanaṁ dukkhaṁ, appiyānañ-ca dassanaṁ.

211 Tasmā piyaṁ na kayi̭rātha, piyāpāyo hi pāpako.
Ganthā tesaṁ na vijjanti yesaṁ natthi piyāppiyaṁ.

212 Piyato jāyatī soko, piyato jāyatī bhayaṁ,
piyato vippamuttassa natthi soko, kuto bhayaṁ?

213 Pemato jāyatī soko, pemato jāyatī bhayaṁ,
pemato vippamuttassa natthi soko, kuto bhayaṁ?

214 Ratiyā jāyatī soko, ratiyā jāyatī bhayaṁ,
ratiyā vippamuttassa natthi soko, kuto bhayaṁ?

16

The Chapter about Love

209 Engaging oneself in what is not suitable,
not engaging in what is suitable,
abandoning the good, grasping the loved,
he envies the one who endeavours for himself.

210 Do not associate at any time with those who are loved
or with those unloved,
there is suffering not meeting those loved, and (suffering from)
meeting those unloved.

211 Therefore do not hold (anything) as loved,
for losing those who are loved is loathsome.
There are no knots for those who hold nothing as loved
or as unloved.

212 From love there arises grief, from love there arises fear,
for one who is free from love there is no grief, how is there fear?

213 From fondness there arises grief, from fondness there arises fear,
for one who is free from fondness there is no grief,
how is there fear?

214 From delight there arises grief, from delight there arises fear,
for one who is free from delight there is no grief, how is there fear?

215 Kāmato jāyatī soko, kāmato jāyatī bhayaṁ,
kāmato vippamuttassa natthi soko, kuto bhayaṁ?

216 Taṇhāya jāyatī soko, taṇhāya jāyatī bhayaṁ,
taṇhāya vippamuttassa natthi soko, kuto bhayaṁ?

217 Sīladassanasampannaṁ, dhammaṭṭhaṁ saccavedinaṁ,
attano kamma' kubbānaṁ, taṁ jano kurute piyaṁ.

218 Chandajāto anakkhāte, manasā ca phuṭo siyā,
kāmesu ca appaṭibaddhacitto, "uddhaṁsoto" ti vuccati.

219⌉ Cirappavāsiṁ purisaṁ dūrato sotthim-āgataṁ,
ñātimittā suhajjā ca abhinandanti āgataṁ.

220⌋ Tatheva katapuññam-pi asmā lokā paraṁ gataṁ,
puññāni paṭigaṇhanti piyaṁ ñātīva āgataṁ.

Piyavaggo Soḷasamo

215 From desire there arises grief, from desire there arises fear,
for one who is free from desire there is no grief, how is there fear?

216 From craving there arises grief, from craving there arises fear,
for one who is free from craving there is no grief, how is there fear?

217 Endowed with virtue and insight, principled, knowing the truths,
doing the deeds that are his own, that one the people love.]

218 The one with desire arisen for the undeclared,
  will be suffused with the (awakening) mind,
with a mind unconnected with sense pleasures,
  he is spoken of as "one gone upstream".

219⌉ When one who lives abroad for a long time comes safely from afar,
his relatives, friends, and companions come and greatly rejoice.

220⌋ Just so, when one who has performed merit goes from this world
  unto the next,
his merits are received just as relatives come to their loved one.

The Chapter about Love, the Sixteenth

17
Kodhavaggo

221 Kodhaṁ jahe, vippajaheyya mānaṁ,
saṁyojanaṁ sabbam-atikkameyya,
taṁ nāmarūpasmiṁ asajjamānaṁ,
akiñcanaṁ nānupatanti dukkhā.

222 Yo ve uppatitaṁ kodhaṁ rathaṁ bhantaṁ va dhāraye,
tam-ahaṁ sārathiṁ brūmi rasmiggāho itaro jano.

223 Akkodhena jine kodhaṁ, asādhuṁ sādhunā jine,
jine kadariyaṁ dānena, saccenālikavādinaṁ.

224 Saccaṁ bhaṇe, na kujjheyya, dajjāppasmim-pi yācito,
etehi tīhi ṭhānehi gacche devāna' santike.

225 Ahiṁsakā ye munayo, niccaṁ kāyena saṁvutā,
te yanti accutaṁ ṭhānaṁ, yattha gantvā na socare.

17
The Chapter about Anger

221 One should abandon anger, one should abandon conceit,
one should overcome every fetter,
without clinging to mind and bodily form,
sufferings never do befall the one having no possessions.

222 Whoever should hold back arisen anger
just like a swerving chariot,
that one I say is a charioteer, other people are just rein-holders.

223 Through kindness one should overcome anger,
through goodness one should overcome a lack of goodness,
through gifts one should overcome stinginess,
through truth (one should overcome) lying speech.

224 One should speak out the truth, one should not get angry,
when requested give, if only a little,
through these three conditions one can go to the presence
of the gods.

225 Those sages without violence, constantly restrained in body,
go to the deathless (Nirvāṇa), having gone there they do not grieve.

226 Sadā jāgaramānānaṁ, ahorattānusikkhinaṁ,
Nibbānaṁ adhimuttānaṁ, atthaṁ gacchanti āsavā.

227 Porāṇam-etaṁ, Atula, netaṁ ajjatanām-iva:
nindanti tuṇhim-āsīnaṁ, nindanti bahubhāṇinaṁ,
mitabhāṇim-pi nindanti, natthi loke anindito.

228 Na cāhu na ca bhavissati, na cetarahi vijjati
ekantaṁ nindito poso, ekantaṁ vā pasaṁsito.

229⌉ Yañ-ce viññū pasaṁsanti, anuvicca suve suve,
acchiddavuttiṁ medhāviṁ, paññāsīlasamāhitaṁ,

230⌋ nekkhaṁ jambonadasseva, ko taṁ ninditum-ar̭ahati?
Devā pi naṁ pasaṁsanti, Brahmunā pi pasaṁsito.

231 Kāyappakopaṁ rakkheyya, kāyena saṁvuto siyā,
kāyaduccaritaṁ hitvā, kāyena sucaritaṁ care.

232 Vacīpakopaṁ rakkheyya, vācāya saṁvuto siyā,
vacīduccaritaṁ hitvā, vācāya sucaritaṁ care.

226 For those who are always wakeful,
who train both by day and by night,
who are intent on Nirvāṇa, the pollutants are laid to rest.

227 This is something of old, Atula, this is not something of today:
they blame the one who sits silently,
they blame the one who talks a lot,
they blame the one who talks in moderation,
there is no one in the world not blamed.

228 There was not and there will not be,
and at present there is not found
a person totally blameworthy, or one totally praiseworthy.

229⌉ The one who, after being examined day by day,
is praised by the wise,
faultless in conduct, sagacious, attending to virtue and wisdom,

230⌋ one who is like a golden coin, who is there worthy to blame him?
That one is praised by the gods,
and has been praised by the Brahmās too.

231 One should guard against bodily anger,
one should be restrained bodily,
abandoning wrong bodily conduct,
one should have good bodily conduct.

232 One should guard against verbal anger,
one should be restrained verbally,
abandoning wrong verbal conduct,
one should have good verbal conduct.

233 Manopakopaṁ rakkheyya, manasā saṁvuto siyā,
manoduccaritaṁ hitvā, manasā sucaritaṁ care.

234 Kāyena saṁvutā dhīrā, atho vācāya saṁvutā,
manasā saṁvutā dhīrā, te ve suparisaṁvutā.

Kodhavaggo Sattarasamo

233 One should guard against mental anger,
one should be restrained mentally,
abandoning wrong mental conduct,
one should have good mental conduct.

234 The wise are restrained bodily, then they are restrained verbally,
the wise are restrained mentally,
they are indeed very well-restrained.

The Chapter about Anger, the Seventeenth

18

Malavaggo

235 Paṇḍupalāso va dāni 'si,
Yamapurisā pi ca taṁ upaṭṭhitā,
uyyogamukhe ca tiṭṭhasi,
pātheyyam-pi ca te na vijjati.

236 So karohi dīpam-attano,
khippaṁ vāyama paṇḍito bhava,
niddhantamalo, anaṅgaṇo,
dibbaṁ ariyabhūmim-ehisi.

237 Upanītavayo ca dāni 'si,
sampayāto 'si Yamassa santike,
vāso pi ca te natthi antarā,
pātheyyam-pi ca te na vijjati.

238 So karohi dīpam-attano,
khippaṁ vāyama paṇḍito bhava,
niddhantamalo anaṅgaṇo,
na punaṁ jātijaraṁ upehisi.

239 Anupubbena medhāvī, thokathokaṁ khaṇe khaṇe,
kammāro rajatasseva, niddhame malam-attano.

18
The Chapter about Stains

235 You are now like a withered leaf,
Yama's men stand waiting for you,
you stand at decay's door,
with no provisions for the journey found.

236 One should make an island for oneself,
soon the wise one should endeavour,
removing the stain, blemishless,
you will go to the divine and noble realm.

237 You are now advanced in age,
you have come to Yama's presence,
there is nowhere to dwell in between,
with no provisions for the journey found.

238 One should make an island for oneself,
soon the wise one should endeavour,
removing the stain, blemishless,
you will not come to birth and old age again.

239 The sage gradually, little by little, moment by moment,
should remove the stain from himself,
like a smith (removes the stain) from silver.

240 Ayasā va malaṁ samuṭṭhitaṁ,
taduṭṭhāya tam-eva khādati,
evaṁ atidhonacārinaṁ—
sakakammāni nayanti duggatiṁ.

241 Asajjhāyamalā mantā, anuṭṭhānamalā gharā,
malaṁ vaṇṇassa kosajjaṁ, pamādo rakkhato malaṁ.

242⌉ Malitthiyā duccaritaṁ, maccheraṁ dadato malaṁ,
malā ve pāpakā dhammā asmiṁ loke paramhi ca.

243⌋ Tato malā malataraṁ, avijjā paramaṁ malaṁ,
etaṁ malaṁ pahatvāna, nimmalā hotha, bhikkhavo!

244 Sujīvaṁ ahirikena, kākasūrena dhaṁsinā,
pakkhandinā pagabbhena, saṅkiliṭṭhena jīvitaṁ.

245 Hirīmatā ca dujjīvaṁ, niccaṁ sucigavesinā,
alīnenāpagabbhena, suddhājīvena passatā.

246⌉ Yo pāṇam-atipāteti, musāvādañ-ca bhāsati,
loke adinnaṁ ādiyati, paradārañ-ca gacchati,

247⌋ surāmerayapānañ-ca yo naro anuyuñjati,
idhevam-eso lokasmiṁ mūlaṁ khaṇati attano.

248 Evaṁ bho purisa jānāhi, pāpadhammā asaññatā,
mā taṁ lobho adhammo ca ciraṁ dukkhāya randhayuṁ.

240 As a (rust) stain arises from iron,
and arisen from that, it eats it away,
so with one who is overindulgent—
his deeds lead him to a bad destiny.

241 Lack of repetition is the ruin of chants,
a lack of maintenance is the ruin of homes,
indolence is the ruin of one's appearance,
heedlessness is the ruin of the one on guard.

242⌉ Bad conduct is a woman's stain, stinginess is a giver's stain,
wicked actions are indeed stains both in this world and in the next.

243⌋ A stain that is worse than that stain,
ignorance is the supreme stain,
after abandoning that stain, be without stains, O monastics!

244 Life is light for one without shame,
with the bold courage of a crow,
living a life with backbiting, recklessness, and defilements.

245 Life is hard when endowed with shame,
for the one constantly seeking purity,
for one sincere, and not reckless, looking for purity of life.

246⌉ Whoever kills a living being, and speaks a word that is not true,
takes what is not given here, and goes to another's wife,

247⌋ that person who is devoted to a drink of liquor and wine,
digs up his own root right here in the world.

248 Know it thus, dear sir, a lack of restraint is a bad thing,
let not greed and corruption oppress you with suffering
for a long time.

249 Dadāti ve yathāsaddhaṁ, yathāpasādanaṁ jano,
tattha yo maṅku bhavati paresaṁ pānabhojane
na so divā vā rattiṁ vā, samādhiṁ adhigacchati.

250 Yassa cetaṁ samucchinnaṁ, mūlaghaccaṁ samūhataṁ,
sa ve divā vā rattiṁ vā, samādhiṁ adhigacchati.

251 Natthi rāgasamo aggi, natthi dosasamo gaho,
natthi mohasamaṁ jālaṁ, natthi taṇhāsamā nadī.

252 Sudassaṁ vajjam-aññesaṁ, attano pana duddasaṁ,
paresaṁ hi so vajjāni opuṇāti yathā bhusaṁ,
attano pana chādeti, kaliṁ va kitavā saṭho.

253 Paravajjānupassissa niccaṁ ujjhānasaññino,
āsavā tassa vaḍḍhanti, ārā so āsavakkhayā.

254 Ākāse va padaṁ natthi, samaṇo natthi bāhire,
papañcābhiratā pajā, nippapañcā Tathāgatā.

255 Ākāse va padaṁ natthi, samaṇo natthi bāhire,
saṅkhārā sassatā natthi, natthi Buddhānam-iñjitaṁ.

Malavaggo Aṭṭhārasamo

249 The people give according to faith, according to their confidence,
herein the one who becomes dejected because of food and drink
(given) to others
he does not, either by day or night attain to (good) concentration.

250 For the one in whom this (dejection) is cut off,
destroyed at the root, dug up,
does, by day and night, attain to (good) concentration.

251 There is no fire that is like passion,
there is nothing that takes a hold like hatred,
there is no snare like delusion, there is no flood like craving.

252 Easy to see are others' fault, but one's own is hard to see,
for one sifts other peoples' faults like they were chaff,
but conceals one's own (faults),
like a crafty cheat (conceals) his defeat.

253 The one who constantly looks for another's fault,
who is an abject complainer,
for him the pollutants increase, he is far from their destruction.

254 There is no footprint in the sky, there is no ascetic on the outside,
folk greatly delight in impediments,
the Realized Ones are free of impediments.

255 There is no footprint in the sky, there is no ascetic on the outside,
there are no constant conditions,
there is no disturbance for the Buddhas.

The Chapter about Stains, the Eighteenth

19
Dhammaṭṭhavaggo

256 Na tena hoti Dhammaṭṭho yenatthaṁ sahasā naye,
yo ca atthaṁ anatthañ-ca ubho niccheyya paṇḍito.

257 Asāhasena dhammena samena nayatī pare,
Dhammassa gutto medhāvī, Dhammaṭṭho ti pavuccati.

258 Na tena paṇḍito hoti yāvatā bahu bhāsati;
khemī averī abhayo, paṇḍito ti pavuccati.

259 Na tāvatā Dhammadharo yāvatā bahu bhāsati,
yo ca appam-pi sutvāna, Dhammaṁ kāyena passati,
sa ve Dhammadharo hoti, yo Dhammaṁ nappamajjati.

260 Na tena thero hoti yenassa palitaṁ siro,
paripakko vayo tassa moghajiṇṇo ti vuccati.

19

The Chapter about One who stands by the Dharma

256 One who would hastily settle a case because of that
  is not one who stands by the Dharma,
the wise one should discriminate the two:
  what is the case and what is not the case.

257 The one who settles for other people without haste,
  justly and impartially,
the sagacious one, protecting the Dharma,
  is said to be one who stands by the Dharma.

258 One is not a wise person merely because of speaking much;
being safe, hatred-free, fearless, one is called a wise person.

259 One is not a Dharma-bearer merely through speaking much,
but the one who, having heard a little, sees the Dharma for himself,
is one who bears the Dharma,
  the one who is not heedless regarding the Dharma.

260 One is not an elder because one's head has grey hair,
for the one who is (only) well-matured, aged,
  is said to be old in vain.

261 Yamhi saccañ-ca Dhammo ca ahiṁsā saṁyamo damo,
sa ve vantamalo dhīro thero iti pavuccati.

262⌝ Na vākkaraṇamattena vaṇṇapokkharatāya vā
sādhurūpo naro hoti, issukī maccharī saṭho;

263⌟ yassa cetaṁ samucchinnaṁ, mūlaghaccaṁ samūhataṁ,
sa vantadoso medhāvī sādhurūpo ti vuccati.

264 Na muṇḍakena samaṇo, abbato alikaṁ bhaṇaṁ,
icchālobhasamāpanno, samaṇo kiṁ bhavissati?

265 Yo ca sameti pāpāni, aṇuṁ-thūlāni sabbaso—
samitattā hi pāpānaṁ samaṇo ti pavuccati.

266 Na tena bhikkhu hoti yāvatā bhikkhate pare,
vissaṁ Dhammaṁ samādāya bhikkhu hoti na tāvatā.

267 Yodha puññañ-ca pāpañ-ca bāhetvā brahmacariyavā,
saṅkhāya loke carati sa ce, bhikkhū ti vuccati.

268 Na monena munī hoti mūḷharūpo aviddasu,
yo ca tulaṁ va paggayha, varam-ādāya paṇḍito.

269 Pāpāni parivajjeti sa munī tena so muni,
yo munāti ubho loke muni tena pavuccati.

261 In whom is truth, the Dharma, non-violence, restraint,
and (good) training,
the wise one who throws out the stain is (truly) called an elder.

262⌉ Not by eloquence only, or by a beautiful complexion,
is a person honourable, (if still) jealous, selfish, and deceitful;

263⌋ for the one in whom this is cut off, destroyed at the root, dug up,
that sage who has thrown out hatred is said to be honourable.

264 Not through a shaven head is one an ascetic,
(if) one lacks vows, speaks lies,
and is endowed with greed and desire, how will one be an ascetic?

265 The one who pacifies wicked deeds, small and great,
in every way—
through the pacifying of wicked deeds he is said to be an ascetic.

266 One is not a monastic merely through eating others' almsfood,
the one who undertakes a false Dharma to that extent
is not a monastic.

267 ° If he is one who lives the holy life here,
warding off both merit and demerit,
and wanders with discrimination in the world,
that one is said to be a monastic.

268 Not through silence is a deluded fool (considered to be) a seer,
the wise one, like one holding the balance, takes up what is noble.

269 The seer who rejects wicked deeds through that
is (considered) a seer,
whoever understands both worlds because of that
is said to be a seer.

270 Na tena ariyo hoti yena pāṇāni hiṁsati,
ahiṁsā sabbapāṇānaṁ ariyo ti pavuccati.

271 Na sīlabbatamattena, bāhusaccena vā pana,
atha vā samādhilābhena, vivittasayanena vā,

272 phusāmi nekkhammasukhaṁ, aputhujjanasevitaṁ;
bhikkhu vissāsa' māpādi appatto āsavakkhayaṁ.

Dhammaṭṭhavaggo Ekūnavīsatimo

270 Not through hurting breathing beings one is noble,
the one who does not hurt any breathing beings is said to be noble.

271 Not merely through virtue or vows, or through great learning,
or through the attainment of concentration,
or through a secluded dwelling,

272 do I attain the happiness of renunciation,
not practised by worldly people;
let a monastic not be confident
(as long as) the destruction of the pollutants is unattained.

The Chapter about the one who stands by the Dharma, the Nineteenth

20

Maggavaggo

273 Maggānaṭṭhaṅgiko seṭṭho, saccānaṁ caturo padā,
virāgo seṭṭho dhammānaṁ, dipadānañ-ca Cakkhumā.

274 Eso va maggo natthañño, dassanassa visuddhiyā,
etaṁ hi tumhe paṭipajjatha, Mārassetaṁ pamohanaṁ.

275 Etaṁ hi tumhe paṭipannā dukkhassantaṁ karissatha,
akkhāto ve mayā maggo, aññāya sallasanthanaṁ.

276 Tumhehi kiccaṁ ātappaṁ akkhātāro Tathāgatā,
paṭipannā pamokkhanti jhāyino Mārabandhanā.

277 Sabbe saṅkhārā aniccā ti, yadā paññāya passati,
atha nibbindatī dukkhe— esa maggo visuddhiyā.

278 Sabbe saṅkhārā dukkhā ti, yadā paññāya passati,
atha nibbindatī dukkhe— esa maggo visuddhiyā.

279 Sabbe dhammā anattā ti, yadā paññāya passati,
atha nibbindatī dukkhe— esa maggo visuddhiyā.

20
The Chapter about the Path

273 The eightfold is the best of paths,
four principles (the best) of truths,
passionlessness the best of states, the Visionary (the best) of men.

274 This is the path, there is no other, for insight and for purity,
you should enter upon this path, this is the confounding of Māra.

275 Having entered upon this path you will make an end to suffering,
the path was declared by me,
the removal of the dart by knowledge.

276 Your duty is to have ardour declare the Realized Ones,
entering this path meditators will be released
from the bonds of Māra.

277 All conditions are impermanent, when one sees this with wisdom,
then one grows tired of suffering—this is the path to purity.

278 All conditions are suffering, when one sees this with wisdom,
then one grows tired of suffering—this is the path to purity.

279 All components (of mind and body) are without self,
when one sees this with wisdom,
then one grows tired of suffering—this is the path to purity.

280 Uṭṭhānakālamhi anuṭṭhahāno,
yuvā balī, ālasiyaṁ upeto,
saṁsannasaṅkappamano kusīto—
paññāya maggaṁ alaso na vindati.

281 Vācānurakkhī manasā susaṁvuto,
kāyena ca akusalaṁ na kayirā,
ete tayo kammapathe visodhaye,
ārādhaye maggaṁ isippaveditaṁ.

282 Yogā ve jāyatī bhūri, ayogā bhūrisaṅkhayo,
etaṁ dvedhāpathaṁ ñatvā bhavāya vibhavāya ca,
tathattānaṁ niveseyya yathā bhūri pavaḍḍhati.

283 Vanaṁ chindatha mā rukkhaṁ, vanato jāyatī bhayaṁ,
chetvā vanañ-ca vanathañ-ca, nibbanā hotha bhikkhavo.

284 Yāva hi vanatho na chijjati
aṇumatto pi narassa nārisu,
paṭibaddhamano va tāva so,
vaccho khīrapako va mātari.

285 Ucchinda sineham-attano,
kumudaṁ sāradikaṁ va pāṇinā,
santimaggam-eva brūhaya
Nibbānaṁ Sugatena desitaṁ.

286 "Idha vassaṁ vasissāmi, idha hemantagimhisu",
iti bālo vicinteti, antarāyaṁ na bujjhati.

280 The one who has not energy at a time for energy,
youthful, strong, (but) given to laziness,
whose mind lacks (right) intention and is indolent—
the lazy one does not find wisdom's path.

281 Verbally guarded, well-restrained in mind,
not doing a wrong deed with the body,
one should purify these three paths of action,
one should undertake the path shown by seers.

282 From effort arises wisdom, without effort wisdom is destroyed,
having understood these two paths of development and decline,
one should establish oneself so that one's wisdom increases.

283 Cut down the forest (of defilements) not just a tree,
from the forest arises a danger,
having cut down the forest and thicket,
you should be without forests, monastics.

284 ° For as long as an atom of desire
of a man for a woman is not cut down,
for just so long is the mind in bondage,
like a calf (in bondage) to mother's milk.

285 Cut off (any) affection for one's self,
like an autumn lotus (plucked) with the hand,
develop fully the path to peace and
Nirvāṇa taught by the Fortunate One.

286 "Here I will dwell during the rains,
here during winter and summer",
in just such a way a fool thinks, not understanding the danger.

287 Taṁ puttapasusammattaṁ byāsattamanasaṁ naraṁ,
suttaṁ gāmaṁ mahogho va maccu ādāya gacchati.

288 Na santi puttā tāṇāya, na pitā na pi bandhavā,
Antakenādhipannassa natthi ñātisu tāṇatā.

289 Etam-atthavasaṁ ñatvā, paṇḍito sīlasaṁvuto,
Nibbānagamanaṁ maggaṁ khippam-eva visodhaye.

Maggavaggo Vīsatimo

287 That person whose mind is attached and besotted
by cattle and children,
is snatched away by death just as a sleeping village (by) a great flood.

288 Children are not a refuge, nor fathers, not even kin,
for one overcome by the End-Maker there is no refuge in relatives.

289 Understanding the truth of this the wise one, endowed with virtue,
should quickly purify the path that is leading to Nirvāṇa.

The Chapter about the Path, the Twentieth

21

Pakiṇṇakavaggo

290 Mattāsukhapariccāgā, passe ce vipulaṁ sukhaṁ,
caje mattāsukhaṁ dhīro, sampassaṁ vipulaṁ sukhaṁ.

291 Paradukkhūpadānena attano sukham-icchati,
verasaṁsaggasaṁsaṭṭho, verā so na parimuccati.

292 Yaṁ hi kiccaṁ tad-apaviddhaṁ, akiccaṁ pana kayirati,
unnalānaṁ pamattānaṁ, tesaṁ vaḍḍhanti āsavā.

293 Yesañ-ca susamāraddhā niccaṁ kāyagatā sati
akiccaṁ te na sevanti, kicce sātaccakārino,
satānaṁ sampajānānaṁ, atthaṁ gacchanti āsavā.

294 Mātaraṁ pitaraṁ hantvā, rājāno dve ca khattiye,
raṭṭhaṁ sānucaraṁ hantvā, anīgho yāti brāhmaṇo.

295 Mātaraṁ pitaraṁ hantvā, rājāno dve ca sotthiye,
veyyagghapañcamaṁ hantvā, anīgho yāti brāhmaṇo.

21
The Miscellaneous Chapter

290 If, by renouncing a small good, he might see a good that is large,
the wise one should renounce that small good,
  seeing the good that is extensive.

291 One who desires happiness for oneself
  by causing suffering for another,
being associated thus with hatred,
  is not fully released from that hatred.

292 That to be done is rejected, but what is not to be done is done,
for the insolent, the heedless, their pollutants increase.

293 But for those who always properly undertake mindfulness
  of the body
who do not practice what is not to be done,
  persisting in what is to be done,
for those mindful ones, those fully aware,
  the pollutants are laid to rest.

294 Destroying mother and father, and (then) two noble kings,
destroying a kingdom and its followers,
  the brahmin proceeds untroubled.

295 Destroying mother and father, and two prosperous kings,
destroying a tiger as the fifth, the brahmin proceeds untroubled.

296 Suppabuddhaṁ pabujjhanti sadā Gotamasāvakā,
yesaṁ divā ca ratto ca niccaṁ Buddhagatā sati.

297 Suppabuddhaṁ pabujjhanti sadā Gotamasāvakā,
yesaṁ divā ca ratto ca niccaṁ Dhammagatā sati.

298 Suppabuddhaṁ pabujjhanti sadā Gotamasāvakā,
yesaṁ divā ca ratto ca niccaṁ Saṅghagatā sati.

299 Suppabuddhaṁ pabujjhanti sadā Gotamasāvakā,
yesaṁ divā ca ratto ca niccaṁ kāyagatā sati.

300 Suppabuddhaṁ pabujjhanti sadā Gotamasāvakā,
yesaṁ divā ca ratto ca ahiṁsāya rato mano.

301 Suppabuddhaṁ pabujjhanti sadā Gotamasāvakā
yesaṁ divā ca ratto ca bhāvanāya rato mano.

302 Duppabbajjaṁ durabhiramaṁ, durāvāsā gharā dukhā,
dukkhosamānasaṁvāso, dukkhānupatitaddhagū,
tasmā na caddhagū siyā, na ca dukkhānupatito siyā.

303 Saddho sīlena sampanno yasobhogasamappito,
yaṁ yaṁ padesaṁ bhajati, tattha tattheva pūjito.

112

296 Gotama's disciples always awake to a good wakening,
those who day and night constantly have mindfulness of the Buddha.

297 Gotama's disciples always awake to a good wakening,
those who day and night constantly have mindfulness of the Dharma.

298 Gotama's disciples always awake to a good wakening,
those who day and night constantly have mindfulness of the Saṅgha.

299 Gotama's disciples always awake to a good wakening,
those who day and night constantly have mindfulness of the body.

300 Gotama's disciples always awake to a good wakening,
those who day and night have a mind that delights in non-violence.

301 Gotama's disciples always awake to a good wakening,
those who day and night have a mind that delights in cultivation.

302 The going forth is hard, it is hard to find delight (therein),
(but) it is (also) hard to dwell in households that are suffering,
dwelling together with those different is suffering,
travellers (in the round of births) are affected by suffering,
therefore do not be a traveller, do not be affected by suffering.

303 The faithful one who is endowed with virtue,
and has wealth and fame,
whatever district he resorts to, right there and then he is worshipped.

304 Dūre santo pakāsenti, himavanto va pabbato,
asantettha na dissanti, rattiṁ khittā yathā sarā.

305 Ekāsanaṁ ekaseyyaṁ, eko caram-atandito,
eko damayam-attānaṁ vanante ramito siyā.

Pakiṇṇakavaggo Ekavīsatimo

304 The good are visible from far, like a mountain covered in snow,
(but) the wicked are not seen here, just like arrows shot in the night.

305 Sitting alone, lying down alone, walking alone, diligent,
the solitary one who trains himself will delight in the edge of a forest.

The Miscellaneous Chapter, the Twenty-First

22

Nirayavaggo

306 Abhūtavādī nirayaṁ upeti,
yo vāpi katvā "Na karomī" ti cāha,
ubho pi te pecca samā bhavanti
nihīnakammā manujā parattha.

307 Kāsāvakaṇṭhā bahavo pāpadhammā asaññatā,
pāpā pāpehi kammehi nirayaṁ te upapajjare.

308 Seyyo ayoguḷo bhutto tatto, aggisikhūpamo,
yañ-ce bhuñjeyya dussīlo raṭṭhapiṇḍaṁ asaññato.

309 Cattāri ṭhānāni naro pamatto,
āpajjatī paradārūpasevī:
apuññalābhaṁ, nanikāmaseyyaṁ,
nindaṁ tatīyaṁ, nirayaṁ catutthaṁ.

310 Apuññalābho ca gatī ca pāpikā,
bhītassa bhītāya ratī ca thokikā,
rājā ca daṇḍaṁ garukaṁ paṇeti,
tasmā naro paradāraṁ na seve.

22
The Chapter about the Underworld

306 The one who speaks falsely goes to the underworld,
and he who says: "I do not do" what he has done,
both of these are just the same when they have gone
to the hereafter, (they are) humans who did base deeds.

307 Many wearing the monastic robe around their necks are wicked, unrestrained,
the wicked through their wicked deeds re-arise in the underworld.

308 It's better to have eaten a glowing iron ball, like a flame of fire,
than that (the monastic) who is unrestrained and unvirtuous should enjoy the country's almsfood.

309 There are four states the man who is heedless,
the man who consorts with other man's wives, undergoes:
he gains demerit, an uncomfortable bed,
blame as third, and (rebirth in) the underworld as fourth.

310 Gaining demerit and a bad destiny,
and (only) the small delight of a scared man with a scared woman,
and kings who apply heavy punishment,
a man therefore should not consort with another's wife.

311 Kuso yathā duggahito hattham-evānukantati,
sāmaññaṁ dupparāmaṭṭhaṁ nirayāyupakaḍḍhati.

312 Yaṁ kiñci sithilaṁ kammaṁ saṅkiliṭṭhañ-ca yaṁ vataṁ,
saṅkassaraṁ brahmacariyaṁ na taṁ hoti mahapphalaṁ.

313 Kayirañ-ce kayirāthenaṁ, daḷham-enaṁ parakkame,
saṭhilo hi paribbājo bhiyyo ākirate rajaṁ.

314 Akataṁ dukkataṁ seyyo, pacchā tapati dukkataṁ,
katañ-ca sukataṁ seyyo, yaṁ katvā nānutappati.

315 Nagaraṁ yathā paccantaṁ guttaṁ santarabāhiraṁ,
evaṁ gopetha attānaṁ, khaṇo vo mā upaccagā,
khaṇātītā hi socanti nirayamhi samappitā.

316 Alajjitāye lajjanti, lajjitāye na lajjare,
micchādiṭṭhisamādānā sattā gacchanti duggatiṁ.

317 Abhaye bhayadassino, bhaye cābhayadassino,
micchādiṭṭhisamādānā sattā gacchanti duggatiṁ.

318 Avajje vajjamatino, vajje cāvajjadassino,
micchādiṭṭhisamādānā sattā gacchanti duggatiṁ.

311 As jagged grass, wrongly grasped, cuts into the hand,
so does the ascetic life, wrongly grasped,
drag one down to the underworld.

312 Whatever lax deed there is and that vow which is defiled,
(know that) a holy life that is doubtful does not have great fruit
for that one.

313 If he would do what should be done, he should be firm in his effort,
for the wanderer who is lax spreads a lot of impurity.

314 Better undone is a wrong-doing, a wrong-doing one later regrets,
better done is what is well-done, which, when done,
one does not regret.

315 As a border town is guarded on the inside and the outside,
so one should watch over oneself, and you should not let the
moment pass,
for when the chance has passed they grieve
when consigned to the underworld.

316 They are ashamed of what is not shameful,
not ashamed of what is shameful,
undertaking wrong views, beings go to a bad destiny.

317 Seeing fear in what is not fearful, not seeing fear in what is fearful,
undertaking wrong views, beings go to a bad destiny.

318 Finding blame in what is blameless,
not seeing blame in what is blameable,
undertaking wrong views, beings go to a bad destiny.

319 Vajjañ-ca vajjato ñatvā, avajjañ-ca avajjato,
sammādiṭṭhisamādānā sattā gacchanti suggatiṁ.

Nirayavaggo Dvāvīsatimo

319 Knowing blame in what is blameable,
and no blame in what is blameless,
undertaking right views, beings go to a good destiny.

The Chapter about the Underworld, the Twenty-Second

23

Nāgavaggo

320 Ahaṁ nāgo va saṅgāme cāpāto patitaṁ saraṁ
ativākyaṁ titikkhissaṁ, dussīlo hi bahujjano.

321 Dantaṁ nayanti samitiṁ, dantaṁ rājābhirūhati,
danto seṭṭho manussesu, yotivākyaṁ titikkhati.

322 Varam-assatarā dantā, ājānīyā ca Sindhavā,
kuñjarā ca mahānāgā, attadanto tato varaṁ.

323 Na hi etehi yānehi gaccheyya agataṁ disaṁ,
yathattanā sudantena, danto dantena gacchati.

324 Dhanapālak nāma kuñjaro
kaṭukappabhedano dunnivārayo,
baddho kabalaṁ na bhuñjati,
sumarati nāgavanassa kuñjaro.

23
The Chapter about the Elephant

320 Like an elephant in battle (endures) an arrow shot from bow
(so) will I endure abuse, for many people are unvirtuous.

321 They lead one trained into a crowd,
a king mounts one who has been trained,
amongst humans one trained is best, the one who can endure abuse.

322 Noble are the well-trained horses, the well-bred horses from Sindh,
and the great tusker elephants, (and even) more noble than that
is the one who has trained himself.

323 Not by these vehicles can one go to the place beyond destinations,
as one through training himself well, being trained by the training,
goes.

324 The tusker named Dhanapālaka
musty in rut, difficult to restrain,
bound, he doesn't eat (even) a morsel,
the tusker remembers the elephant forest.

325 Middhī yadā hoti mahagghaso ca,
niddāyitā samparivattasāyī,
mahāvarāho va nivāpapuṭṭho,
punappunaṁ gabbham-upeti mando.

326 Idaṁ pure cittam-acāri cārikaṁ
yenicchakaṁ yatthakāmaṁ yathāsukhaṁ,
tad-ajjahaṁ niggahessāmi yoniso,
hatthim-pabhinnaṁ viya aṅkusaggaho.

327 Appamādaratā hotha, sacittam-anurakkhatha,
duggā uddharathattānaṁ paṅke sanno va kuñjaro.

328 Sace labhetha nipakaṁ sahāyaṁ
saddhiṁcaraṁ sādhuvihāridhīraṁ,
abhibhuyya sabbāni parissayāni
careyya tenattamano satīmā.

329 No ce labhetha nipakaṁ sahāyaṁ
saddhiṁcaraṁ sādhuvihāridhīraṁ,
rājā va raṭṭhaṁ vijitaṁ pahāya
eko care mātaṅgaraññe va nāgo.

330 Ekassa caritaṁ seyyo, natthi bāle sahāyatā,
eko care na ca pāpāni kayirā,
appossukko mātaṅgaraññe va nāgo.

331 Atthamhi jātamhi sukhā sahāyā,
tuṭṭhī sukhā yā itarītarena,
puññaṁ sukhaṁ jīvitasaṅkhayamhi,
sabbassa dukkhassa sukhaṁ pahāṇaṁ.

325 When one is torpid and overeats,
sleepy and rolling on the bed,
like a great pig fed on fodder,
that fool comes to the womb again.

326 Formerly this wandering mind wandered
through desire, pleasure, and happiness,
(but) today I will control it wisely,
like one with goad an elephant in rut.

327 You should delight in heedfulness,
you should always protect your mind,
you should raise yourself from this pit like the tusker sunk in the mud.

328 If you should find a prudent friend
or companion, one who lives well, a wise one,
overcoming all your troubles
you should live with that one, glad and mindful.

329 If you do not find a prudent friend
or companion, one who lives well, a wise one,
like a king who abandons his conquered kingdom
one should live alone like a solitary elephant in the forest.

330 It is better to live alone, there can be no friendship with a fool,
one should live alone and not do anything bad,
unconcerned like a solitary elephant in the forest.

331 Friends are good whenever need arises,
being content with everything is good,
at the break-up of life merit is good,
the abandoning of all suffering is good.

332 Sukhā matteyyatā loke, atho petteyyatā sukhā,
sukhā sāmaññatā loke, atho brahmaññatā sukhā.

333 Sukhaṁ yāva jarā sīlaṁ, sukhā saddhā patiṭṭhitā,
sukho paññāya paṭilābho, pāpānaṁ akaraṇaṁ sukhaṁ.

Nāgavaggo Tevīsatimo

332 Respecting one's mother is good in the world,
also respecting one's father is good,
respecting ascetics is good in the world,
also respecting (true) brahmins is good.

333 Virtuous conduct till old age is good,
the establishing of faith is good,
the acquisition of wisdom is good, doing nothing wicked is good.

The Chapter about the Elephant, the Twenty-Third

24

Taṇhāvaggo

334 Manujassa pamattacārino
taṇhā vaḍḍhati māluvā viya,
so palavatī hurāhuraṁ
phalam-icchaṁ va vanasmi' vānaro.

335 Yaṁ esā sahatī jammī taṇhā loke visattikā,
sokā tassa pavaḍḍhanti abhivaṭṭhaṁ va bīraṇaṁ.

336 Yo cetaṁ sahatī jammiṁ taṇhaṁ loke duraccayaṁ,
sokā tamhā papatanti udabindu va pokkharā.

337 Taṁ vo vadāmi: "Bhaddaṁ vo yāvantettha samāgatā",
taṇhāya mūlaṁ khaṇatha, usīrattho va bīraṇaṁ,
mā vo naḷaṁ va soto va Māro bhañji punappunaṁ.

338 Yathā pi mūle anupaddave daḷhe
chinno pi rukkho, punar-eva rūhati,
evam-pi taṇhānusaye anūhate
nibbattatī dukkham-idaṁ punappunaṁ.

24
The Chapter about Craving

334 For a human who lives life heedlessly
craving increases like a clinging creeper,
he rushes from one place to another
like a monkey desiring fruit in the forest.

335 That one who is overcome by these low cravings and attachments
in the world,
for him griefs increase like grass that has had heavy rain.

336 Whoever overcomes this low craving in the world,
which is difficult to get past,
griefs fall from him like a drop of water from a lotus.

337 This I say to you: "Good luck to as many as have assembled here",
dig up the root of craving, like one seeking the root (digs up) grass,
do not let Māra push you down again
like a stream (pushes down) the reed.

338 Just as when the root remains firm and untroubled
though the tree was cut down, it grows again,
so when the tendency to craving is not rooted out
this suffering appears again and again.

339 Yassa chattiṁsatī sotā manāpassavanā bhusā,
vāhā vahanti duddiṭṭhiṁ saṅkappā rāganissitā.

340 Savanti sabbadhī sotā, latā ubbhijja tiṭṭhati,
tañ-ca disvā lataṁ jātaṁ mūlaṁ paññāya chindatha.

341 Saritāni sinehitāni ca
sŏmanassāni bhavanti jantuno,
te sātasitā sukhesino,
te ve jātijarūpagā narā.

342 Tasiṇāya purakkhatā pajā
parisappanti saso va bādhito,
saṁyojanasaṅgasattakā
dukkham-upenti punappunaṁ cirāya.

343 Tasiṇāya purakkhatā pajā
parisappanti saso va bādhito,
tasmā tasiṇaṁ vinodaye—
bhikkhu ākaṅkha' virāgam-attano.

344 Yo nibbanatho vanādhimutto,
vanamutto vanam-eva dhāvati,
taṁ puggalam-etha passatha,
mutto bandhanam-eva dhāvati.

345[1] Na taṁ daḷhaṁ bandhanam-āhu dhīrā,
yad-āyasaṁ dārujaṁ pabbajañ-ca,
sārattarattā maṇikuṇḍalesu
puttesu dāresu ca yā apekhā—

339 He in whom the thirty-six streams flow pleasantly and strong,
the one with wrong view is carried away
by his passionate intentions.

340 Streams are flowing everywhere,
the creepers remain where they grow,
seeing this, cut the creeper's root that has arisen with wisdom.

341 ° There are flowing streams of affection and
mental happinesses for a person,
pleasure-dependent they seek happiness,
those people undergo birth and old age.

342 People surrounded by craving
crawl round like a hare in a trap,
attached and clinging to fetters
they come back again and again to suffering for a long time.

343 People surrounded by craving
crawl round like a hare in a trap,
therefore he should remove craving—
the monk who longs for dispassion for himself.

344 The one who is free from desires, who is intent on the forest,
(though) free from the forest, runs back to the forest,
come here and look at that person,
(though) free, he runs back to bondage.

345[1] That bondage is not so strong say the wise,
that is made of iron or wood or reeds,
° impassioned and excited they seek out
jewels and earrings and children and wives—

346⌋ etaṁ daḷhaṁ bandhanam-āhu dhīrā,
ohārinaṁ sithilaṁ, duppamuñcaṁ,
etam-pi chetvāna paribbajanti
anapekkhino, kāmasukhaṁ pahāya.

347 Ye rāgarattānupatanti sotaṁ
sayaṁkataṁ makkaṭako va jālaṁ,
etam-pi chetvāna vajanti dhīrā,
anapekkhino sabbadukkhaṁ pahāya.

348 Muñca pure, muñca pacchato,
majjhe muñca, bhavassa pāragū,
sabbattha vimuttamānaso,
na punaṁ jātijaraṁ upehisi.

349 Vitakkapamathitassa jantuno
tibbarāgassa, subhānupassino,
bhiyyo taṇhā pavaḍḍhati,
esa kho daḷhaṁ karoti bandhanaṁ.

350 Vitakkupasame ca yo rato
asubhaṁ bhāvayatī sadā sato,
esa kho vyantikāhiti,
esacchecchati Mārabandhanaṁ.

351 Niṭṭhaṁ gato asantāsī, vītataṇho anaṅgaṇo,
acchindi bhavasallāni, antimoyaṁ samussayo.

346 that bondage is strong say the wise,
dragging down the lax, hard to get free from,
having cut this down they wander about
seeking nothing, abandoning the happiness in pleasure.

347 Those who are impassioned by passion follow the stream
like a spider a web made by itself,
having cut this away the wise proceed,
seeking nothing, abandoning all suffering.

348 Be free of the past, be free of the future,
be free of the present, after crossing over (all) existence,
with mind liberated in every way,
you will not return to birth and old age.

349 For a person crushed by thoughts
and pierced by passion, contemplating the attractive,
craving increases much more,
this surely makes the bond more firm.

350 Whoever has delight in the calming of thoughts,
who always mindfully cultivates what is unattractive,
will surely abolish this (craving),
he will cut off the bond of Māra.

351 Having gone to the end, without trembling, without craving,
without impurity,
cutting off the darts of existence, this one is his final body.

352 Vītataṇho anādāno, niruttipadakovido,
akkharānaṁ sannipātaṁ jaññā pubbaparāni ca,
sa ve antimasārīro mahāpañño (mahāpuriso) ti vuccati.

353 Sabbābhibhū sabbavidūham-asmi,
sabbesu dhammesu anūpalitto,
sabbañjaho taṇhakkhaye vimutto,
sayaṁ abhiññāya, kam-uddiseyyaṁ.

354 Sabbadānaṁ Dhammadānaṁ jināti,
sabbaṁ rasaṁ Dhammaraso jināti,
sabbaṁ ratiṁ Dhammaratiṁ jināti,
taṇhakkhayo sabbadukkhaṁ jināti.

355 Hananti bhogā dummedhaṁ no ve pāragavesino,
bhogataṇhāya dummedho hanti aññe va attanaṁ.

356 Tiṇadosāni khettāni, rāgadosā ayaṁ pajā,
tasmā hi vītarāgesu dinnaṁ hoti mahapphalaṁ.

357 Tiṇadosāni khettāni, dosadosā ayaṁ pajā,
tasmā hi vītadosesu dinnaṁ hoti mahapphalaṁ.

352 Without craving, without attachment,
  skilled in words and their explanation,
knowing how syllables are arranged,
  which come before and which after,
the one in his final body is said to be (a great person),
  one of great wisdom.

353 All-Conquering, All-Wise am I,
undefiled regarding all things,
having given up everything, liberated through craving's destruction,
when having deep knowledge myself, who should I point to
  (as Teacher)?

354 The gift of the Dharma surpasses all other gifts,
the taste of the Dharma surpasses all other tastes,
the love of the Dharma surpasses all other loves,
destruction of craving overcomes all suffering.

355 Riches destroy the stupid one who does not seek the way beyond,
through his craving for riches the stupid one destroys others
  and himself.

356 Fields are ruined by grassy weeds, these people are ruined by passion,
therefore there is great fruit for that given to those without passion.

357 Fields are ruined by grassy weeds, these people are ruined by hatred,
therefore there is great fruit for that given to those without hatred.

358 Tiṇadosāni khettāni, mohadosā ayaṁ pajā,
tasmā hi vītamohesu dinnaṁ hoti mahapphalaṁ.

359 Tiṇadosāni khettāni, icchādosā ayaṁ pajā,
tasmā hi vigaticchesu dinnaṁ hoti mahapphalaṁ.

Taṇhāvaggo Catuvīsatimo

358 Fields are ruined by grassy weeds, these people are ruined
by delusion,
therefore there is great fruit for that given to those without delusion.

359 Fields are ruined by grassy weeds, these people are ruined by desire,
therefore there is great fruit for that given to those without desire.

The Chapter about Craving, the Twenty-Fourth

25

Bhikkhuvaggo

360 Cakkhunā saṁvaro sādhu, sādhu sotena saṁvaro,
ghāṇena saṁvaro sādhu, sādhu jivhāya saṁvaro,

361 kāyena saṁvaro sādhu, sādhu vācāya saṁvaro,
manasā saṁvaro sādhu, sādhu sabbattha saṁvaro,
sabbattha saṁvuto bhikkhu sabbadukkhā pamuccati.

362 Hatthasaṁyatŏ pādasaṁyato,
vācāya saṁyatŏ saṁyatuttamo,
ajjhattarato samāhito,
eko santusito: tam-āhu bhikkhuṁ.

363 Yo mukhasaṁyato bhikkhu, mantabhāṇī anuddhato,
atthaṁ Dhammañ-ca dīpeti, madhuraṁ tassa bhāsitaṁ.

364 Dhammārāmo Dhammarato, Dhammaṁ anuvicintayaṁ,
Dhammaṁ anussaraṁ bhikkhu, Saddhammā na parihāyati.

25
The Chapter about Monastics

360⌉ Restraint of eye is good, restraint of ear is good,
restraint of nose is good, restraint of tongue is good,

361⌋ restraint of body is good, restraint of speech is good,
restraint of mind is good, restraint is everywhere good,
a monastic who is restrained everywhere
  is liberated from all suffering.

362 One who controls his hands, controls his feet,
controls his speech, controls the (mind) supreme,
with inner delight and composure,
solitary, content: that one is called a monastic.

363 That monastic who restrains the mouth, who speaks well,
  and who is modest,
who explains the meaning of the Dharma, his speech is sweet.

364 The one who finds pleasure in the Dharma, delights in the Dharma,
  reflects on the Dharma,
the monastic who remembers the Dharma, does not abandon
  the Good Dharma.

365 Salābhaṁ nātimaññeyya, nāññesaṁ pihayaṁ care,
aññesaṁ pihayaṁ bhikkhu samādhiṁ nādhigacchati.

366 Appalābho pi ce bhikkhu salābhaṁ nātimaññati,
taṁ ve devā pasaṁsanti suddhājīviṁ atanditaṁ.

367 Sabbaso nāmarūpasmiṁ yassa natthi mamāyitaṁ,
asatā ca na socati, sa ve bhikkhū ti vuccati.

368 Mettāvihārī yo bhikkhu, pasanno Buddhasāsane,
adhigacche padaṁ santaṁ, saṅkhārūpasamaṁ sukhaṁ.

369 Siñca bhikkhu imaṁ nāvaṁ, sittā te lahum-essati,
chetvā rāgañ-ca dosañ-ca, tato Nibbānam-ehisi.

370 Pañca chinde, pañca jahe, pañca cuttaribhāvaye,
pañca saṅgātigo bhikkhu oghatiṇṇo ti vuccati.

371 Jhāya, bhikkhu, mā ca pāmado,
mā te kāmaguṇe bhamassu cittaṁ,
mā lohaguḷaṁ gilī, pamatto,
mā kandi: "Dukkham-idan"-ti ḍayhamāno.

372 Natthi jhānaṁ apaññassa, paññā natthi ajhāyato,
yamhi jhānañ-ca paññā ca sa ve Nibbānasantike.

365 One should not despise one's own gains,
one should not live envious of others,
the monastic who is envious of others does not attain concentration.

366 Even if a monastic gains little he should not despise his gains,
even the very gods praise the one of pure life who is diligent.

367 The one who does not have fondness at all for mind and body,
and who grieves not for what does not exist,
is surely called a monastic.

368 That monastic who dwells in loving-kindness, with faith in Buddha's dispensation,
should attain the state of peace, the joy in stilling of (all) conditions.

369 Please bail out this boat, monastic, when bailed out it will go lightly,
cutting off passion and hatred, from here one will go to Nirvāṇa.

370 One should cut off five, one should abandon five,
one should cultivate five more,
the monastic who surmounts five attachments
is called a flood-crosser.

371 Meditate, monastic, do not be heedless,
do not let your mind swirl around in strands of desire,
do not, heedless, swallow a (hot) iron ball,
do not, while burning, cry: "This is suffering."

372 There is no concentration for one without wisdom,
there is no wisdom for one without concentration,
the one who has both concentration and wisdom
is indeed in the presence of Nirvāṇa.

373 Suññāgāraṁ paviṭṭhassa, santacittassa bhikkhuno,
amānusī ratī hoti sammā Dhammaṁ vipassato.

374 Yato yato sammasati khandhānaṁ udayabbayaṁ
labhatī pītipāmojjaṁ, amataṁ taṁ vijānataṁ.

375 Tatrāyam-ādi bhavati idha paññassa bhikkhuno:
indriyagutti santuṭṭhī, pātimokkhe ca saṁvaro.

376 Mitte bhajassu kalyāṇe suddhājīve atandite,
paṭisanthāravuttassa ācārakusalo siyā,
tato pāmojjabahulo, dukkhassantaṁ karissati.

377 Vassikā viya pupphāni maddavāni pamuñcati,
evaṁ rāgañ-ca dosañ-ca vippamuñcetha bhikkhavo.

378 Santakāyo santavāco, santavā susamāhito,
vantalokāmiso bhikkhu upasanto ti vuccati.

379 Attanā codayattānaṁ, paṭimāsettam-attanā,
so attagutto satimā sukhaṁ bhikkhu vihāhisi.

380 Attā hi attano nātho, attā hi attano gati,
tasmā saṁyamayattānaṁ assaṁ bhadraṁ va vāṇijo.

373 For the one who has entered an empty place,
  a monastic with a peaceful mind,
there is superhuman delight from insight into the true Dharma.

374 Whoever has right mindfulness regarding the rise and fall
  of the components (of mind and body)
gains joy and happiness, that is the deathless state
  for the one who knows.

375 This is the very beginning for the wise monastic here:
contentment, guarding the senses, and restraint in the regulations.

376 One should resort to spiritual friends, ones of pure life,
  ones who are diligent,
one should be of friendly disposition,
  one who will be skilful in his conduct,
rejoicing frequently because of that, one will make an end
  to suffering.

377 Just as striped jasmine casts off its withered flowers,
so, monastics, cast off (all) passion and hatred.

378 Calm in body and calm in speech, having calmness and composure,
having thrown off worldly gain the monastic is called one at peace.

379 By oneself one should censure self,
  by oneself one should be controlled,
he who guards himself, mindful, will live happily, monastic.

380 Self is the protector of self, self is the refuge of self,
therefore one should restrain oneself,
  as a merchant his noble horse.

381 Pāmojjabahulo bhikkhu, pasanno Buddhasāsane,
adhigacche padaṁ santaṁ, saṅkhārūpasamaṁ sukhaṁ.

382 Yo have daharo bhikkhu yuñjati Buddhasāsane,
sŏ imaṁ lokaṁ pabhāseti, abbhā mutto va candimā.

Bhikkhuvaggo Pañcavīsatimo

381 The monastic, having much happiness,
with faith in the dispensation of the Buddha,
could attain to the state of peace,
happy in the stilling of (all) conditions.

382 That young monastic who is devoted to the Buddha's dispensation,
shines forth in this world, like the moon freed from a cloud.

The Chapter about Monastics, the Twenty-Fifth

26

Brāhmaṇavaggo

383 Chinda sotaṁ parakkamma, kāme panuda, brāhmaṇa,
saṅkhārānaṁ khayaṁ ñatvā, akataññūsi, brāhmaṇa.

384 Yadā dvayesu dhammesu pāragū hoti brāhmaṇo,
athassa sabbe saṁyogā atthaṁ gacchanti jānato.

385 Yassa pāraṁ apāraṁ vā pārāpāraṁ na vijjati,
vītaddaraṁ visaṁyuttaṁ, tam-ahaṁ brūmi brāhmaṇaṁ.

386 Jhāyiṁ virajam-āsīnaṁ, katakiccaṁ anāsavaṁ,
uttamatthaṁ anuppattaṁ, tam-ahaṁ brūmi brāhmaṇaṁ.

387 Divā tapati ādicco, rattiṁ ābhāti candimā,
sannaddho khattiyo tapati, jhāyī tapati brāhmaṇo,
atha sabbam-ahorattiṁ Buddho tapati tejasā.

388 Bāhitapāpo ti brāhmaṇo,
samacariyā samaṇo ti vuccati,
pabbājayam-attano malaṁ
tasmā pabbajito ti vuccati.

26

The Chapter about Brahmins

383 Strive and cut off the stream, remove desire, brahmin,
knowing the destruction of the conditioned,
be one who knows that which is not made, brahmin.

384 When a brahmin has, through two things, crossed over,
then, for one who knows, all the fetters are laid to rest.

385 For whom the near shore, the far shore, or both do not exist,
free of anxiety, being detached, that one I say is a brahmin.

386 The meditator sitting down, the one who is dustless,
who has done his duty, without pollutants,
who has reached the ultimate good, that one I say is a brahmin.

387 The sun is radiant by day, the moon shines by night,
the accoutred noble is radiant, the meditating brahmin is radiant,
yet every day and night the Buddha is radiant through his power.

388 Warding off wickedness one is called a brahmin,
one living austerely is said to be an ascetic,
° because of driving forth (all) stain from oneself
one is said to be one who has gone forth.

389 Na brāhmaṇassa pahareyya, nāssa muñcetha brāhmaṇo,
dhī brāhmaṇassa hantāraṁ, tato: dhī yassa muñcati.

390 Na brāhmaṇass' etad-akiñci seyyo:
yadā nisedho manaso piyehi,
yato yato hiṁsamano nivattati,
tato tato sammati-m-eva dukkhaṁ.

391 Yassa kāyena vācāya manasā natthi dukkataṁ,
saṁvutaṁ tīhi ṭhānehi, tam-ahaṁ brūmi brāhmaṇaṁ.

392 Yamhā Dhammaṁ vijāneyya Sammāsambuddhadesitaṁ,
sakkaccaṁ taṁ namasseyya, aggihuttaṁ va brāhmaṇo.

393 Na jaṭāhi na gottena, na jaccā hoti brāhmaṇo,
yamhi saccañ-ca Dhammo ca, so sucī so va brāhmaṇo.

394 Kiṁ te jaṭāhi dummedha, kiṁ te ajinasāṭiyā?
Abbhantaraṁ te gahanaṁ, bāhiraṁ parimajjasi.

395 Paṁsukūladharaṁ jantuṁ, kisaṁ dhamanisanthataṁ,
ekaṁ vanasmiṁ jhāyantaṁ, tam-ahaṁ brūmi brāhmaṇaṁ.

396 Na cāhaṁ brāhmaṇaṁ brūmi yonijaṁ mattisambhavaṁ,
bhovādī nāma so hoti sace hoti sakiñcano;
akiñcanaṁ anādānaṁ, tam-ahaṁ brūmi brāhmaṇaṁ.

389 A brahmin should not hit a brahmin, nor should he abandon him,
woe to one who strikes a brahmin, further: woe to one who lets fly.

390 It is no little good for the brahmin:
when the mind is held back from what is dear,
whenever his mind turns back from violence,
then there is a calming of suffering.

391 For whom there is no wrong-doing bodily, verbally, or mentally,
being restrained in (these) three things, that one I say is a brahmin.

392 That one from whom one learned the Dharma
taught by the Perfect Sambuddha,
with respect bow down to him,
like a brahmin (bows) at fire-sacrifice.

393 Not because of matted hair, family, or birth is one a true brahmin,
in whom there is truth and Dharma, that one is pure,
that one is surely a brahmin.

394 Why do you have your hair matted, stupid one,
and why your deer-skin?
Within you there is a jungle, you (only) polish the outside.

395 That one who wears discarded clothes, who is lean
with protruding veins,
who meditates alone in the forest, that one I say is a brahmin.

396 I do not call one a brahmin simply because of being born
from a (certain) womb,
that one is just one who says "bho" if he is attached;
having nothing and unattached, that one I say is a brahmin.

397 Sabbasaṁyojanaṁ chetvā yo ve na paritassati,
saṅgātigaṁ visaṁyuttaṁ, tam-ahaṁ brūmi brāhmaṇaṁ.

398 Chetvā naddhiṁ varattañ-ca, sandānaṁ sahanukkamaṁ,
ukkhittapalighaṁ buddhaṁ, tam-ahaṁ brūmi brāhmaṇaṁ.

399 Akkosaṁ vadhabandhañ-ca aduṭṭho yo titikkhati,
khantībalaṁ balānīkaṁ, tam-ahaṁ brūmi brāhmaṇaṁ.

400 Akkodhanaṁ vatavantaṁ, sīlavantaṁ anussutaṁ,
dantaṁ antimasārīraṁ, tam-ahaṁ brūmi brāhmaṇaṁ.

401 Vāri pokkharapatte va, āragge-r-iva sāsapo,
yo na lippati kāmesu, tam-ahaṁ brūmi brāhmaṇaṁ.

402 Yo dukkhassa pajānāti idheva khayam-attano,
pannabhāraṁ visaṁyuttaṁ, tam-ahaṁ brūmi brāhmaṇaṁ.

403 Gambhīrapaññaṁ medhāviṁ, maggāmaggassa kovidaṁ,
uttamatthaṁ anuppattaṁ, tam-ahaṁ brūmi brāhmaṇaṁ.

404 Asaṁsaṭṭhaṁ gahaṭṭhehi anāgārehi cūbhayaṁ,
anokasāriṁ appicchaṁ, tam-ahaṁ brūmi brāhmaṇaṁ.

405 Nidhāya daṇḍaṁ bhūtesu tasesu thāvaresu ca,
yo na hanti na ghāteti, tam-ahaṁ brūmi brāhmaṇaṁ.

406. Aviruddhaṁ viruddhesu, attadaṇḍesu nibbutaṁ,
sādānesu anādānaṁ, tam-ahaṁ brūmi brāhmaṇaṁ.

397 Whoever has cut off all the fetters surely does not tremble,
surmounting attachments, detached, that one I say is a brahmin.

398 (Whoever) has cut off the thong, the strap, the rope,
together with the bridle,
who has thrown off the obstacle and is awakened,
that one I say is a brahmin.

399 Whoever, being pure, forbears with punishment, bondage,
and abuse,
having the strength of endurance, having an army of strengths,
that one I say is a brahmin.

400 (Whoever is) controlled of mind, dutiful, virtuous, taint-free,
well-trained and in his last body, that one I say is a brahmin.

401 Like water on the lotus leaf, like a mustard seed on a needle,
he who is unsmeared by desires, that one I say is a brahmin.

402 Whoever knows right here the destruction of his suffering,
putting down the burden, detached, that one I say is a brahmin.

403 The deeply wise sagacious one, skilled in what is path and not path,
who has reached the ultimate good, that one I say is a brahmin.

404 (Whoever) doesn't mix with either householders or the houseless,
wandering homeless, with few desires, that one I say is a brahmin.

405 ° Whoever has laid down the stick (used)
against fearful and fearless beings,
who neither hurts nor kills, that one I say is a brahmin.

406 Being friendly with the hostile, calm amongst those holding a stick,
not attached amongst those attached, that one I say is a brahmin.

407 Yassa rāgo ca doso ca māno makkho ca pātito,
sāsapo-r-iva āraggā, tam-ahaṁ brūmi brāhmaṇaṁ.

408 Akakkasaṁ viññapaniṁ giraṁ saccaṁ udīraye,
yāya nābhisaje kañci, tam-ahaṁ brūmi brāhmaṇaṁ.

409 Yodha dīghaṁ va rassaṁ vā aṇuṁ-thūlaṁ subhāsubhaṁ,
loke adinnaṁ nādiyati, tam-ahaṁ brūmi brāhmaṇaṁ.

410 Āsā yassa na vijjanti asmiṁ loke paramhi ca,
nirāsayaṁ visaṁyuttaṁ, tam-ahaṁ brūmi brāhmaṇaṁ.

411 Yassālayā na vijjanti, aññāya akathaṅkathī,
amatogadhaṁ anuppattaṁ, tam-ahaṁ brūmi brāhmaṇaṁ.

412 Yodha puññañ-ca pāpañ-ca ubho saṅgaṁ upaccagā,
asokaṁ virajaṁ suddhaṁ, tam-ahaṁ brūmi brāhmaṇaṁ.

413 Candaṁ va vimalaṁ suddhaṁ, vippasannam-anāvilaṁ,
nandībhavaparikkhīṇaṁ, tam-ahaṁ brūmi brāhmaṇaṁ.

414 Yo imaṁ palipathaṁ duggaṁ saṁsāraṁ moham-accagā,
tiṇṇo pāragato jhāyī, anejo akathaṅkathī,
anupādāya nibbuto, tam-ahaṁ brūmi brāhmaṇaṁ.

415 Yodha kāme pahatvāna anāgāro paribbaje,
kāmabhavaparikkhīṇaṁ, tam-ahaṁ brūmi brāhmaṇaṁ.

407 Whoever has dropped off passion and hatred, conceit, and anger,
like a mustard seed from a needle, that one I say is a brahmin.

408 (Whoever) speaks a word of truth that is informed and is not coarse,
through which no one would be angry, that one I say is a brahmin.

409 ° Whoever in the world does not take what is not given, long, short,
small, large, attractive, or unattractive, that one I say is a brahmin.

410 For the one who has no longings in this world or in the next world,
being without longings, detached, that one I say is a brahmin.

411 For the one who has no desires, who, through knowledge,
is without doubt,
who has reached immersion in the deathless,
that one I say is a brahmin.

412 Whoever here has overcome clinging to both merit and demerit,
who is griefless, dustless, and pure, that one I say is a brahmin.

413 (Whoever) just like the moon is stainless, pure, clear,
and undisturbed,
has destroyed joy in existence, that one I say is a brahmin.

414 He who has crossed the difficult and dangerous path
through births and deaths and delusion,
the meditator who has crossed over to the further shore,
free of lust and free of doubt,
unattached and cooled down, that one I say is a brahmin.

415 Whoever, giving up sensual desires, would wander homeless here,
destroying desires and existence, that one I say is a brahmin.

416 Yodha taṇhaṁ pahatvāna, anāgāro paribbaje,
taṇhābhavaparikkhīṇaṁ, tam-ahaṁ brūmi brāhmaṇaṁ.

417 Hitvā mānusakaṁ yogaṁ, dibbaṁ yogaṁ upaccagā,
sabbayogavisaṁyuttaṁ, tam-ahaṁ brūmi brāhmaṇaṁ.

418 Hitvā ratiñ-ca aratiñ-ca, sītibhūtaṁ nirūpadhiṁ,
sabbalokābhibhuṁ vīraṁ, tam-ahaṁ brūmi brāhmaṇaṁ.

419 Cutiṁ yo vedi sattānaṁ upapattiñ-ca sabbaso,
asattaṁ sugataṁ buddhaṁ, tam-ahaṁ brūmi brāhmaṇaṁ.

420 Yassa gatiṁ na jānanti devā gandhabbamānusā—
khīṇāsavaṁ Arahantaṁ, tam-ahaṁ brūmi brāhmaṇaṁ.

421 Yassa pure ca pacchā ca majjhe ca natthi kiñcanaṁ,
akiñcanaṁ anādānaṁ, tam-ahaṁ brūmi brāhmaṇaṁ.

422 Usabhaṁ pavaraṁ vīraṁ, mahesiṁ vijitāvinaṁ,
anejaṁ nhātakaṁ buddhaṁ, tam-ahaṁ brūmi brāhmaṇaṁ.

423 Pubbenivāsaṁ yo vedī, saggāpāyañ-ca passati,
atho jātikkhayaṁ patto, abhiññāvosito muni,
sabbavositavosānaṁ, tam-ahaṁ brūmi brāhmaṇaṁ.

Brāhmaṇavaggo Chabbīsatimo

Dhammapadaṁ Niṭṭhitaṁ

416 Whoever, giving up craving, would wander homeless here,
destroying craving and existence, that one I say is a brahmin.

417 Abandoning the human yoke, overcoming the divine yoke,
being unattached to all yokes, that one I say is a brahmin.

418 Abandoning delight and aversion, cooled off and free from cleaving,
a hero who vanquished the whole world, that one I say is a brahmin.

419 Whoever knows in every way beings' passing and their rebirth,
unattached, fortunate, awake, that one I say is a brahmin.

420 For the one whose destiny is unknown to gods, gandharvas,
and men—
being pollutant-free, an Arhat, that one I say is a brahmin.

421 For whom there is nothing in the past, the future, or the present,
having nothing and unattached, that one I say is a brahmin.

422 A noble leader, heroic, a great seer, victorious,
free of lust, cleansed and awakened, that one I say is a brahmin.

423 Whoever knows their former lives,
and sees heaven and the downfall,
and has attained birth's destruction, the sage,
accomplished in deep knowledge,
who is accomplished in all accomplishments,
that one I say is a brahmin.

The Chapter about Brahmins, the Twenty-Sixth

The Dharma Verses are Finished

www.ingramcontent.com/pod-product-compliance
Lightning Source LLC
Chambersburg PA
CBHW021108090426
42738CB00006B/552
* 9 7 8 1 7 8 2 0 1 2 5 8 0 *